Australia's wonderful climate creates the incentive for barbecue cookery ... with our great weather and the abundance of first-rate produce available year round, it's no wonder we love to cook outdoors! *The Essential Barbecue Cookbook* provides dozens of innovative recipes, many designed for a covered barbecue so you can roast, smoke and even bake out of doors. But no matter how y... ...we feel there's enough inspi... ...he heat!

the
essential
barbecue
cookbook

Contents

Mustard honey glazed vegetables, page 92

Ginger tuna with wasabi drizzle, page 72

Sugar and rosemary smoked rump, page 29

Caramelised peaches with spiced yogurt, page 104

The Essential Barbecue Cookbook...

No longer just a backyard accessory, the barbecue has moved into the mainstream of cookery. As you'll see in these pages, today's new-wave charcoal and gas-fired barbecues perform cooking techniques that will astonish you. With the recipes in this book for baking, smoking and roasting, no matter what the heat source, you're sure to be "cooking with gas"!

BRITISH & NORTH AMERICAN READERS:
Please note that Australian cup and spoon measurements are metric. A quick conversion guide appears on page 119. A glossary explaining unfamiliar terms and ingredients begins on page 112.

We would like to thank the following for their assistance —
Barbeques Galore (Aust) Pty Ltd
Margaret McDonagh, Food Consultant
Rinnai Australia Pty Ltd

Grist for the grill

Gone are the days when you simply placed a sheet of metal over a couple of bricks. Nowadays, you can purchase a barbie to suit every situation, ranging from very basic models right through to top-of-the-range versions featuring everything that opens and shuts. If you haven't already bought one, take the time to shop around and match your needs with the features available. Before you shop, you may wish to decide on what type of barbie you're after – gas or charcoal.

Gas barbecues are instant, clean and easy to control. They are the most popular, as well as the more expensive. Most units have at least two burners, making it possible to cook meat over high direct heat while simultaneously cooking vegetables over low direct heat. Some have a fitted hood, offering the option of cooking with indirect heat.

Charcoal/briquette/wood barbecues suit people who enjoy the flavour and experience of cooking over

a. wood   b. briquettes
c. wood   d. charcoal

charred wood. Although they are cheaper to buy than gas and electric barbecues, they take longer to reach cooking heat and are messy to clean.

Getting to know your gas barbecue

Gas barbecues use one of two types of heat conductor, lava rocks or ceramic rocks, arranged over a mesh framework fitted above the burners.

Lava rocks are porous, medium to large chunks of volcanic rock that absorb heat and add flavour. The rocks can be removed and washed, then dried in sunlight before replacing them in the barbecue.

Ceramic rocks (sometimes called compressed lava rocks) are non-porous, disc or pyramid shapes made from a compound that includes lava rock in its makeup; they hold heat well. Ceramic rocks can be cleaned by turning them cooking-side-down and allowing the gas burners to burn off any residue that collects.

Flame-tamer grids, also known as flavour bars, are designed to reduce flare-ups; they also add an open-fire cooked flavour to food. They are available either as a cast-iron grid or a grid of vitreous enamel-coated movable bars. The vitreous enamel flame-tamer grid takes longer to heat than the cast-iron flame-tamer grid, so preheating times need to be extended if using the former.

Most gas barbecues are fitted with a slide-out draining tray that holds fat soak or fat absorber. The base of the tray should be lined with foil then sprinkled evenly with fat soak or absorber. Check the tray regularly and replace the fat absorber when necessary, as

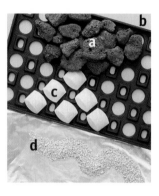

a. lava rocks   b. flame-tamer grid
c. ceramic rocks   d. fat soaker

accumulated fat can cause flare-ups. Most barbecues have a grease receptacle that must be emptied regularly to avoid flare-ups.

Getting to know your charcoal/briquette/wood barbecue

Charcoal, as a heat conductor, is available in hardwood or lumpwood form. Natural charcoal, most commonly made from mesquite or other kinds of hardwood, starts more quickly, burns with about twice the heat of briquettes, and smells cleaner.

Briquettes and heat beads are manufactured from ground charcoal with the addition of a little coal dust and starch to help bind the mixture. Heat beads burn longer than charcoal, but both burn for a reasonable length of time and distribute the heat evenly.

Wood is unpredictable as a heat conductor and difficult to control. It must be lit long before required for cooking to produce the bed of glowing embers that retain enough heat to complete cooking (adding more wood produces flames and smoke, which gives food an unpleasant taste). Treated wood should never be used as a fuel when barbecuing any food.

Cooking tips for charcoal/briquette/wood barbecues

The fire is ready when the coals are covered in a layer of white ash. You should be able to hold your hand about 15cm from the cooking rack for three to four seconds; if you cannot, the fire is too hot. If you can and don't feel any heat after a few seconds, the source has either gone out or it has not yet reached the correct cooking temperature.

Charcoal heat can, to some degree, be controlled manually. To make the fire burn hotter: shake the grill or tap the coals with metal tongs in order to remove accumulated ash. Using metal tongs, push the coals closer together; open all vents; add new/more charcoal. To make the fire burn more slowly: partially close the vents; using metal tongs, push the coals farther apart.

How much charcoal do I use?

For cooking over direct heat, one layer of charcoal should cover an area slightly larger than the food. For indirect heat, use twice the depth of coals, as they will need to burn for a longer time.

Cooking methods

There are two main methods you can use when cooking on a barbecue:

DIRECT HEAT also called direct cooking, direct method or open grill. This is the traditional method, where the food is placed on the barbecue grill or plate and cooked directly over the heat source. This is the best method for sausages, steaks, burgers, vegetables, and so on. A rotisserie may be used with the direct method over low burners (gas) or with an enamel baking dish below the roast (charcoal) to minimise flare-ups. Food can also be wrapped in foil to protect it when using the direct method.

INDIRECT HEAT also called covered cooking or kettle cooking. With gas, the food is placed in a preheated, covered barbecue with the burners directly under the food turned off while the side burners remain on. With charcoal, charcoal rails (metal bars) hold two stacks of coals against the barbecue's sides, leaving the centre of the barbecue rack empty. A disposable aluminium drip tray can be placed here, if desired. The food is cooked by the circulating hot air as well as by the heat conductors. This method of cooking is good for large pieces of food because it ensures the food cooks all the way through without drying out. It is also suitable for smoking and slow-cooking.

You can also use a combination of both methods. Thick steaks or pieces of chicken, for instance, can be seared first using direct heat, then covered and cooked using indirect heat for more even cooking and juice retention.

Smoking

Smoking is a cooking style in which the flavours of the food are affected by the choice of wood used. Hickory and mesquite are the best known woods for smoking; however, there are many different varieties available, such as applewood, tea tree, cherry, peach or banksia.

Wood chips have to be soaked first in cold water so that they will smoulder slowly over the fire, rather than burning. For additional

flavours and scents, soak a variety of herbs and spices in the water along with your choice of wood chips.

Smoking is best suited to moderate-to-slow cooking. Instead of placing the soaked wood chips or chunks and the herbs directly onto the open flame where they burn too rapidly, put them in

a smoke box to combust slowly without causing flare-ups or unnecessary ash. During preheating, place the filled cast-iron smoke box over the heat source. When smoke appears from within the box, adjust the burners on a gas barbecue to low. If using a charcoal barbecue, place the smoke box directly

under the food and use indirect heat.

For the best results when smoking, try not to interrupt cooking with frequent opening or removal of the lid. For this reason, bear in mind that basting too frequently will lessen the intensity of the smoky flavour you want to achieve.

Grist for the grill

Preparation

To correctly "cure" or "season" the cast-iron cooking surface of a gas barbecue, the following steps should be followed. Most of these rules also apply to a cast-iron plate in a charcoal barbecue:

■ Use a light vegetable oil, such as canola, sunflower or safflower oil, and brush or lightly spray all cast-iron surfaces all over (this includes grills, plates, burners and cast-iron rock tray, if you have one).

■ Place cast-iron grill or plate in position, open hood and ignite all burners.

■ Heat barbecue on high, uncovered, until grill or plate begins to smoke.

■ Turn the burners down to low. Fill a bucket with cold water (no detergent); using a stiff wire brush, reserved for the purpose, scrub the grill and plate until clean.

■ Turn burners off. Lightly spray or brush grill and plate with a light vegetable oil. Your barbecue is now ready for you to use.

Caring for your barbecue

Once you have finished cooking on a gas barbecue, never leave it uncleaned. The acidity from the meat fat will, with time, corrode the grill and plate.

Turn all burners to high (if you have a hood, it should remain open during cleaning). When grill or plate begins to smoke, turn gas off at the bottle (to prevent gas build-up in the hose), then at the controls. Using a stiff wire brush and cold water (no detergent), scrub the grill and plate.

Lightly spray or brush the grill or barbecue plate with a light vegetable oil before putting it away, to prevent rusting.

Invest in a vinyl cover to keep your barbecue looking in peak condition.

Dos & don'ts

■ Keep the grill or plate lightly oiled to prevent food sticking.

■ Soak bamboo skewers in water to prevent them scorching during cooking. If using metal skewers, oil them to prevent food from sticking to them.

■ Bring food to room temperature before you start cooking.

■ Trim away excess fat from meat to avoid any flare-ups during cooking.

■ Don't salt meat before cooking, as it draws out the juices. If salt is necessary, add it just before the end of cooking time.

■ Never use an aerosol cooking oil on a barbecue that is alight.

corn husks

aluminium foil

banana leaves

■ When using aluminium foil, always wrap the food with the shiny side towards the food. Banana leaves and corn husks make good wrappers, too.

■ Always use glass or ceramic dishes for marinating food; metal can taint flavours.

■ To avoid burning sugar- or honey-based marinated food, cook over medium rather than high heat.

■ It is best to sear meat on each side over high heat for a few minutes, then move it to a cooler part of the barbecue to continue cooking as desired. Turn meat once only to retain juices and flavour, and to avoid toughening.

■ Use tongs or a slide to turn meat (a fork pierces the meat causing loss of juices). Never cut meat to see if it is cooked; instead, press the meat with tongs – rare feels soft to touch; medium will offer a little resistance; well-done will be firm when pressed.

■ Use a meat thermometer to determine cooking time for larger cuts of meat, but NEVER leave the thermometer in the meat while it's cooking. Insert it towards the end of the cooking time and leave in for a few minutes or until the temperature stabilises.

■ For extra-moist fish, cook whole fish unscaled then, once cooked, peel off the skin and scales. Alternatively, cook scaled fish wrapped in foil.

■ Some sausages and spareribs are best if par-boiled before cooking to prevent excessive fat content causing flare-ups over direct heat. There is no need for par-boiling if cooking using indirect heat. Soaking sausages in an acidic marinade can also help alleviate the need to par-boil or prick them.

■ Don't use charcoal barbecues when it's very windy – flames are hard to control.

■ Make sure the fire is completely extinguished when the barbecue is over.

■ After using a barbecue with a gas cylinder, make sure it is turned off properly to extinguish the flame.

Accessories and additions

■ Gasfuse: essential for safety and convenience when using gas barbecues. An Australian invention that prevents gas leaks and possibly disastrous gas explosions, it is placed between the cylinder bottle and the regulator or hose supply of LP gas cylinders.

■ Roast holder and rack: the upper section of all covered barbecues is hotter than the grill level because of rising heat and the heat absorbed by the hood. Roast holders and racks are great to use to elevate the food from the grill for even cooking and browning. With two prongs that you insert into the food, the rack is an excellent alternative to a rotisserie.

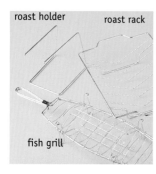

roast holder roast rack

fish grill

■ Fish grill: also known as fish cage or basket. Available in varying sizes to hold different quantities/sizes of fish. Can be used with indirect or direct cooking.

■ Meat thermometer: takes the guesswork out of cooking time, especially for thicker cuts of meat.

■ Firestarters: also called firelighters, are helpful in getting the fire going. Solid blocks or in liquid form.

■ Side burner: great for stir-frying, heating sauces, deep-frying and so on, outdoors.

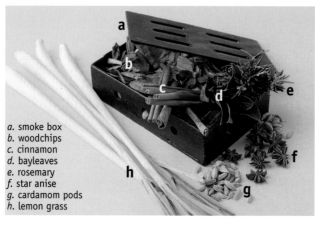

a. smoke box
b. woodchips
c. cinnamon
d. bayleaves
e. rosemary
f. star anise
g. cardamom pods
h. lemon grass

■ Smoke box: a cast-iron box that is filled with smoking chips. Air holes allow a smoky flavour to be imparted to barbecued foods.

■ Smoking chips: available in many different woods; suitable for use in a smoke box or in a baking dish.

vegetable rack

■ Vegetable rack: has prongs for securing vegetables.

■ Stiff wire cleaning brush: ideal for removing charred food from grill or plate.

■ Charcoal chimney: also known as fire-lighting hood and used when lighting charcoal. It is a metal cylinder with a handle and air holes on the side.

■ Barbecue tool set: slides, long-handled tongs, basting brushes, forks, skewers and knives can all be found in barbecue tool sets.

■ Rotisserie: battery-operated rotisseries are available and can be used with both direct and indirect heat. When mounting food on a rotisserie, make sure it is well-centred and properly balanced – uneven weight distribution can place strain on the motor. To avoid flare-ups, cook on rotisserie using indirect heat and place an enamel tray filled with water or wine under the food.

■ Disposable baking dish: for use with indirect heat and smoking. They are usually made of aluminium (or use an inexpensive roasting tray from the supermarket).

■ Barbecue plates and grills: additional plates and grills are available for gas and charcoal barbecues.

disposable baking dish

kebab rack

cast-iron plate

■ Kebab rack: used to elevate food and ensure even cooking and browning.

■ Warming rack: used to keep food warm with direct heat, or to cook food by the indirect heat method.

warming rack

Beef and Veal

From ribs to roasts, rib-eye or rump, we can't think of a single cut of beef or veal that doesn't taste twice as good barbecued as it does when cooked in the house. Meat and the barbie are a match made in heaven... together, it seems, practically since man discovered fire. And it's little wonder – beef's full flavour, its sumptuous juices and seductive aromas are all enlivened by a hearty dash of summer and smoke.

BEEF AND HALOUMI KEBABS WITH CAPER BUTTER

Soak bamboo skewers in water for about 1 hour to prevent them scorching.

1kg rump steak, cubed
2 tablespoons olive oil
1 tablespoon grated lemon rind
2 tablespoons lemon juice
1 tablespoon grated
   fresh horseradish
400g haloumi cheese, cubed
8 medium corn tortillas

CAPER BUTTER
2 tablespoons drained capers,
   chopped finely
100g butter, melted

Place beef in large shallow dish with combined oil, rind, juice and horseradish. *[Best made ahead to this stage. Cover, refrigerate 3 hours or overnight.]*
   Thread beef and cheese on 8 skewers; cook on heated oiled barbecue until browned all over and cooked as desired. Meanwhile, wrap tortillas in foil in parcels of 4 and heat on barbecue. Remove tortillas from foil, wrap each skewer in a tortilla. To serve, remove skewers, if desired, leaving beef and cheese enclosed; accompany with Caper Butter.

Caper Butter Combine capers and butter in small bowl.

SERVES 4

BEEF AND VEGETABLE TEPPAN YAKI

4 (600g) beef fillet steaks
1/4 cup (60ml) Japanese dark
   soy sauce
2 tablespoons mirin
2 tablespoons sake
1 teaspoon grated fresh ginger
2 teaspoons brown sugar
1 clove garlic, crushed
250g snow peas
250g asparagus

Place beef in large bowl with combined soy, mirin, sake, ginger, sugar and garlic. *[Best made ahead to this stage. Cover, refrigerate 3 hours or overnight.]*
   Steam or microwave snow peas and asparagus, separately, until just tender; drain. Drain beef over medium bowl; place vegetables in bowl with reserved marinade. Cook beef on heated oiled barbecue until browned both sides and cooked as desired. Meanwhile, towards end of beef cooking time, drain vegetables; discard marinade. Cook vegetables, alongside beef on barbecue, until browned all over.

SERVES 4

From left Beef and vegetable teppan yaki;
Beef and haloumi kebabs with caper butter

RIB STEAKS WITH CAPSICUM PESTO AND MASHED KUMARA

4 (1.5kg) beef rib steaks (with bone in)

CAPSICUM PESTO

2 large (700g) red capsicums, seeded, quartered
1/2 cup (75g) sun-dried tomatoes in oil, drained
1 tablespoon grated fresh ginger
1 tablespoon olive oil
1 teaspoon sugar
2 tablespoons finely chopped fresh basil leaves

MASHED KUMARA

2 large (1kg) kumara, chopped
1 large (300g) potato, chopped
1/4 cup (60ml) cream
1 clove garlic, crushed
1 teaspoon ground cumin

Cook beef on heated oiled barbecue until browned both sides and cooked as desired. Serve steaks, topped with Capsicum Pesto, on Mashed Kumara.

Capsicum Pesto Blend or process capsicum until almost smooth; strain, discard liquid. Blend or process sun-dried tomatoes, ginger, oil and sugar. Place mixture in medium bowl; stir in capsicum puree and basil.

Mashed Kumara Boil, steam or microwave kumara and potato, separately, until tender; drain. Mash together with cream, garlic and cumin.

SERVES 4

NEW YORK CUT STEAKS IN HERBED MUSHROOM SAUCE

4 (1kg) boneless sirloin steaks (New York cut)
2/3 cup (160ml) dry red wine
1 tablespoon horseradish cream
2 teaspoons finely chopped fresh lemon thyme
1 tablespoon olive oil
1 tablespoon brown sugar
30g butter
1 large (200g) white onion, sliced
1 clove garlic, crushed
500g button mushrooms, sliced
1/4 cup (60ml) beef stock
1 tablespoon chopped fresh parsley

Place beef in large shallow dish with 1/2 cup (125ml) of the wine, 2 teaspoons of the horseradish cream, 1 teaspoon of the thyme, and all of the oil and sugar. *[Best made ahead to this stage. Cover, refrigerate 3 hours or overnight.]*

Cook beef on heated oiled barbecue until browned both sides and cooked as desired. Meanwhile, melt butter in large pan on barbecue; cook onion and garlic, stirring, until onion is soft. Add mushrooms; cook until soft. Add remaining horseradish, thyme and wine with stock; simmer, uncovered, about 5 minutes or until most of the liquid has evaporated. Stir in parsley. Serve beef with herbed mushroom sauce.

SERVES 4

VEAL SHOULDER WITH SPICED COUSCOUS

1 cup (200g) couscous
1 cup (250ml) boiling water
30g butter
1 medium (150g) brown onion, chopped finely
1 clove garlic, crushed
2 teaspoons ground cumin
2 teaspoons ground turmeric
1 tablespoon caraway seeds, toasted
2 tablespoons finely chopped fresh coriander leaves
1/3 cup (80ml) lemon juice
2kg veal shoulder, boned
2 tablespoons olive oil

Combine couscous and measured amount of boiling water in medium heatproof bowl; cover, stand about 5 minutes or until water is absorbed. Using fork, toss couscous to separate grains.

Melt butter in small pan; cook onion and garlic, stirring, until onion is soft. Combine onion mixture with couscous; add cumin, turmeric, caraway, coriander and half the juice. Place veal, cut-side-up, on board. Place couscous mixture in centre of veal; roll tightly, secure with string. *[Best made just before cooking.]*

Place veal in disposable baking dish; drizzle with oil and remaining juice. Cook in covered barbecue, using indirect heat, following manufacturer's instructions, about 40 minutes or until browned all over and cooked as desired.

SERVES 6

Left, from top New York cut steaks in herbed mushroom sauce; Rib steaks with capsicum pesto and mashed kumara
Above Veal shoulder with spiced couscous

BEEF FAJITAS

500g beef fillet, sliced thinly
1/3 cup (80ml) barbecue sauce
1 teaspoon ground cumin
1 teaspoon ground coriander
1/2 teaspoon chilli powder
1 small (150g) red capsicum,
    seeded, sliced
1 small (150g) green capsicum,
    seeded, sliced
1 small (150g) yellow capsicum,
    seeded, sliced
8 large flour tortillas
3/4 cup (180ml) sour cream

AVOCADO TOPPING
2 medium (500g) avocados
1 tablespoon lime juice
1 clove garlic, crushed

TOMATO SALSA
2 medium (380g) tomatoes,
    seeded, chopped
1 small (100g) red onion, chopped
1 tablespoon olive oil
2 teaspoons chopped fresh
    coriander leaves

Place beef in medium bowl with sauce, cumin, coriander and chilli. *[Best made ahead to this stage. Cover, refrigerate for 3 hours or overnight.]*

Cook capsicum slices on heated oiled barbecue plate until browned; remove from barbecue. Cook beef on heated oiled barbecue plate until browned and cooked as desired. Return capsicum to barbecue plate with beef and cook just until hot.

Meanwhile, wrap tortillas in foil in parcels of 4 and heat on barbecue. Remove tortillas from foil and divide beef mixture among them. Top with sour cream, Avocado Topping and Tomato Salsa.

Avocado Topping Mash both avocados coarsely in a medium bowl with a fork; mash in the lime juice and garlic.

Tomato Salsa Combine all ingredients in a small bowl.

SERVES 4

INDIAN SPICED BEEF WITH DHAL

2 tablespoons cumin seeds
1 tablespoon coriander seeds
2 teaspoons sweet paprika
2 teaspoons ground cinnamon
1 teaspoon ground cardamom
1 teaspoon chilli powder
5 cloves garlic, crushed
2 teaspoons grated fresh ginger
1/4 cup (60ml) peanut oil
2kg beef rump roast

DHAL
1 1/2 cups (300g) red lentils
1/4 cup shredded fresh mint leaves
4 cups (1 litre) vegetable stock

Cook cumin and coriander seeds, paprika, cinnamon, cardamom and chilli powder in dry medium pan, stirring, until fragrant. Place seed mixture in small bowl with garlic, ginger and oil; mix to a paste. Trim as much fat from beef as possible; spread paste all over beef. *[Best made ahead to this stage. Cover, refrigerate at least 3 hours or overnight.]*

Place beef on roasting rack or basket, or in disposable baking dish. Cook in covered barbecue, using indirect heat, following manufacturer's instructions, about 1 hour 20 minutes or until browned all over and cooked as desired. Remove from heat, cover; stand 10 minutes before slicing. Serve with Dhal.

Dhal Combine lentils, mint and stock in medium pan. Bring to boil; simmer, uncovered, stirring occasionally, about 15 minutes or until lentils are tender.

SERVES 8

Left Beef fajitas
Above Indian spiced beef with dhal

Bowls from Orson & Blake Collectables

VEAL MEDALLIONS WITH OLIVE PASTE

2 cups (100g) firmly packed fresh
    parsley leaves
1/2 cup (60g) seeded black olives
2 tablespoons (30g) drained capers
1 tablespoon lemon juice
1 clove garlic, crushed
4 (800g) veal eye fillet medallions
8 slices (120g) prosciutto

Blend or process parsley until finely chopped. With motor operating, add olives, capers, juice and garlic; blend until almost smooth. *[Can be made ahead to this stage. Cover, refrigerate up to 1 week.]*

Spread olive mixture around the edge of each medallion; wrap 2 slices prosciutto around each piece to cover olive mixture, secure with toothpicks. Cook veal on heated oiled barbecue until browned both sides and cooked as desired. Just before serving, remove toothpicks.

SERVES 4

VEAL PARMIGIANA

2 teaspoons olive oil
1 medium (150g) white onion,
    chopped finely
2 cloves garlic, crushed
400g can tomatoes
1/4 cup (60ml) tomato paste
1 tablespoon balsamic vinegar
1 teaspoon sugar
1 tablespoon shredded fresh
    basil leaves
2 small (460g) eggplants
8 (960g) veal leg steaks
1 1/2 cups (150g) grated pizza cheese

Heat oil in small pan; cook onion and garlic, stirring, until onion is soft. Add undrained crushed tomatoes, paste, vinegar and sugar; simmer, uncovered, about 10 minutes or until sauce thickens, stir in basil. *[Can be made a day ahead to this stage. Cover, refrigerate overnight.]*

Meanwhile, cut unpeeled eggplants into 1cm slices; cook on heated oiled barbecue until browned both sides. Cook veal on heated oiled barbecue until browned one side. Turn veal, top with sauce, eggplant and cheese; cook until cheese is melted and veal is cooked as desired.

SERVES 4 TO 6

From left Veal parmigiana; Veal medallions with olive paste

VEAL CUTLETS WITH A THREE-BEAN SALAD

1 cup (200g) dried
  black-eyed beans
2 teaspoons cumin seeds
2 teaspoons ground coriander
2 tablespoons chopped fresh
  mint leaves
1/2 cup (125ml) olive oil
4 drained sun-dried tomatoes
  in oil, chopped
1 tablespoon cider vinegar
1 clove garlic, crushed
8 (1.4kg) veal cutlets
150g green beans
1 1/2 cups (230g) frozen broad
  beans, cooked, peeled

Place black-eyed beans in large bowl, cover with water; cover, stand overnight.

Drain beans; place in large pan of boiling water. Simmer, uncovered, for about 30 minutes or until beans are tender; drain. [Can be made ahead to this stage. Cover, refrigerate overnight.]

Add spices to heated dry pan; cook, stirring, until fragrant. Blend or process spices, mint, oil, tomato, vinegar and garlic until smooth. Place cutlets in large bowl with half of the spice mixture. [Can be made ahead to this stage. Cover, refrigerate overnight or freeze.]

Cook cutlets on heated oiled barbecue until browned both sides and cooked as desired. Meanwhile, boil, steam or microwave green beans until tender; drain. Combine all beans with remaining spice mixture in large bowl; serve with cutlets.

SERVES 4

VEAL STEAKS WITH LEMON AND THYME SAUCE

60g butter
1 egg yolk
1 tablespoon sweet chilli sauce
1 teaspoon grated lemon rind
2 tablespoons lemon juice
2 teaspoons chopped fresh thyme
8 (960g) veal leg steaks

Melt butter in small pan; add egg yolk, sauce, rind and juice. Cook, stirring, over low heat, without boiling, until sauce thickens slightly. Stir in thyme; cool. Cover and refrigerate until just set. [Can be made ahead to this stage. Cover, refrigerate overnight.]

Spread half the sauce over both sides of steaks; cook steaks on heated oiled barbecue until browned both sides and cooked as desired. Just before serving, spread steaks with remaining sauce.

SERVES 4 TO 6

BEEF SAUSAGES WITH CARAMELISED ONIONS

Order sausage casing from the butcher.

1kg minced beef
2 cups (140g) stale breadcrumbs
^{1}/$_2$ cup (125ml) dry red wine
^{1}/$_4$ cup (60ml) tomato paste
2 teaspoons chopped fresh oregano
1 teaspoon chopped fresh thyme
1 teaspoon cracked black pepper
2 metres sausage casing

CARAMELISED ONIONS
50g butter
4 large (800g) brown onions, sliced
1 clove garlic, crushed
2 tablespoons brown sugar
1 tablespoon balsamic vinegar
2 tablespoons beef stock

Combine beef, breadcrumbs, wine, paste, herbs and pepper in large bowl. Place half of the beef mixture into large piping bag fitted with 1.5cm plain tube. Tie a knot at one end of sausage casing. Open other end of casing, place over tube; work all of casing onto tube.

Pipe beef mixture into casing, twisting casing at 10cm intervals for individual sausages. Repeat with remaining beef

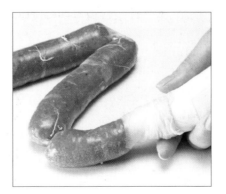

mixture. *[Can be made ahead to this stage. Cover, refrigerate overnight or freeze.]*

Cook sausages on heated oiled barbecue until browned all over and cooked through. Serve with Caramelised Onions.

Caramelised Onions Melt butter in medium pan on barbecue; cook onion and garlic, stirring, until onion is soft and browned. Add sugar, vinegar and stock; cook, stirring, until thick and syrupy.

MAKES ABOUT 20 SAUSAGES

Left, from top Veal cutlets with a three-bean salad; Veal steaks with lemon and thyme sauce
Above Beef sausages with caramelised onions

GREEK-STYLE BEEF WITH TZATZIKI AND SALAD

1/4 cup (60ml) lemon juice
1/4 cup (60ml) olive oil
1/3 cup chopped fresh oregano
2 cloves garlic, crushed
2 tablespoons dry white wine
4 beef T-bone steaks

TZATZIKI
200ml yogurt
1 clove garlic, crushed
2 teaspoons lemon juice
1 medium (170g) cucumber, chopped finely
1/2 teaspoon ground cumin
1 tablespoon chopped fresh mint leaves

GARLIC ROCKET SALAD
1 tablespoon dry white wine
1 tablespoon lemon juice
2 teaspoons olive oil
2 cloves garlic, crushed
250g torn rocket leaves
100g baby spinach leaves

Combine juice, oil, oregano, garlic and wine in large bowl; add beef to marinade. *[Must be made ahead to this stage. Cover, refrigerate 3 hours or overnight.]*

Drain beef; discard marinade. Cook beef on heated oiled barbecue until browned both sides and cooked as desired. Serve with Tzatziki and Garlic Rocket Salad.

Tzatziki Combine all ingredients in small bowl.

Garlic Rocket Salad Combine wine, juice, oil and garlic in jar; shake well. In large bowl gently toss rocket, spinach and dressing.

SERVES 4

JAZZY BEEF SAUSAGES

1/4 cup (60ml) barbecue sauce
1 tablespoon Worcestershire sauce
1 tablespoon tomato sauce
1 clove garlic, crushed
8 thick (920g) beef sausages
2 medium (300g) brown onions, sliced

Combine sauces and garlic in small bowl. Cook sausages and onion on heated oiled barbecue, brushing occasionally with sauce mixture, until browned all over and cooked through.

SERVES 4

NACHOS SAUSAGES

8 thick (920g) beef sausages
50g packet tasty cheese corn chips, crushed coarsely
2/3 cup (160ml) mild chunky salsa
2/3 cup (80g) pizza cheese

Cook sausages on heated oiled barbecue until browned all over and cooked through. Cut a slit down the length of each sausage, not cutting through.

Sprinkle sausages with corn chips, top with salsa and cheese. Return sausages to barbecue, cook until cheese melts.

SERVES 4

SAUSAGES WITH GARLIC MUSHROOMS

50g butter
2 cloves garlic, crushed
150g button mushrooms, sliced
2 teaspoons Dijon mustard
1 tablespoon dry white wine
8 thick (920g) beef sausages

Heat butter in medium pan, add garlic and mushrooms; cook, stirring, until mushrooms are tender and browned lightly. Add mustard and wine, cook, stirring, until nearly all the liquid has evaporated. Cook sausages on heated oiled barbecue until browned all over and cooked through. Serve sausages with garlic mushrooms.

SERVES 4

SAUSAGES WITH MAPLE SYRUP AND MUSTARD

20g butter
1/4 cup (60ml) maple syrup
1 tablespoon Dijon mustard
1/2 cup (125ml) orange juice
12 thin (920g) beef sausages

Combine butter, syrup, mustard and juice in small pan; stir over low heat until ingredients are combined. Cook sausages on heated oiled barbecue, brushing occasionally with maple syrup mixture, until browned all over and cooked through.

SERVES 4

Top, from left Sausages with garlic mushrooms, Nachos sausages, Sausages with maple syrup and mustard, Jazzy beef sausages; Greek-style beef with tzatziki and salad

BEEF WITH SPICED SEA SALT CRUST

2 tablespoons dried juniper berries, chopped
2 tablespoons grated lemon rind
1 tablespoon sea salt flakes
1 tablespoon cracked black pepper
2 teaspoons ground cumin
2kg beef sirloin roast

Combine berries, rind, salt, pepper and cumin in small bowl; press onto beef. *[Best made ahead to this stage. Cover, refrigerate 3 hours or overnight.]*

Place beef on roasting rack or basket, or in disposable baking dish. Cook in covered barbecue, using indirect heat, following manufacturer's instructions, about 1 hour 20 minutes or until browned all over and cooked as desired. Remove from heat, cover; stand 10 minutes before slicing and serving.

SERVES 8 TO 10

BEEF WITH BRANDIED WALNUTS AND PRUNES

650g beef butt fillet
1/3 cup (80ml) walnut oil
1/3 cup (80ml) cider vinegar
1/3 cup (90g) finely chopped palm sugar
11/2 cups (255g) seeded prunes, halved
1 cup (100g) walnuts pieces, chopped coarsely
1/3 cup (80ml) brandy
70g butter

Place beef in large bowl with combined walnut oil, vinegar and sugar. *[Best made ahead to this stage. Cover, refrigerate for 3 hours or overnight.]*

Drain beef over medium pan; reserve marinade. Cook beef on heated oiled barbecue until well browned all over. Place beef on roasting rack or basket, or in disposable baking dish. Cook in covered barbecue, using indirect heat, following manufacturer's instructions, about 40 minutes or until browned all over and cooked as desired. Remove from heat, cover; stand 10 minutes before slicing and serving.

Meanwhile, combine reserved marinade with prunes, nuts, brandy and butter. Bring to boil; simmer, uncovered, for 5 minutes. Serve brandied walnuts and prunes with beef.

SERVES 4

Left from top Beef with spiced sea salt crust; Beef with brandied walnuts and prunes

BURGERS BELLISSIMO

1 large (350g) red capsicum
2 cloves garlic, crushed
1 small (80g) white onion, chopped
1/4 cup (35g) sun-dried tomatoes in
   oil, drained, chopped coarsely
2 tablespoons sun-dried
   tomato pesto
1kg minced beef
200g fetta cheese, crumbled
1 large (300g) red onion, sliced
2 large (500g) tomatoes,
   sliced thickly
8 bread rolls
100g mesclun

AVOCADO DRESSING
1 medium (250g) avocado
1/3 cup (80ml) buttermilk
1 tablespoon lemon juice

Quarter capsicum, remove and discard seeds and membrane. Roast under grill or in very hot oven, skin-side-up, until skin blisters and blackens. Cover capsicum pieces in plastic or paper for 5 minutes; peel away and discard skin, chop flesh roughly. Blend or process capsicum, garlic, white onion, sun-dried tomato and pesto until smooth. Combine vegetable mixture in large bowl with beef; shape mixture into 8 patties. Cover, refrigerate 30 minutes. *[Can be made ahead to this stage. Cover, refrigerate overnight or freeze.]*

Cook patties on heated oiled barbecue until browned one side; turn, sprinkle with cheese, cook until browned and cooked through.

Meanwhile, cook red onion and tomato slices on heated oiled barbecue until onion is browned lightly and tomato browned both sides. Split rolls; toast. Spread bases with some of the Avocado Dressing; top with mesclun, patties, onion and tomato. Drizzle burgers with remaining Dressing.

Avocado Dressing Blend or process all ingredients until smooth. *[Can be made a few hours ahead. Cover, refrigerate.]*

MAKES 8

MEGA BEEF BURGERS

1kg minced beef
1 small (80g) brown onion,
   chopped finely
2 cloves garlic, crushed
2 tablespoons barbecue sauce
2 tablespoons Worcestershire sauce
2 teaspoons all-purpose seasoning
2 tablespoons chopped fresh parsley
1/2 cup (35g) stale breadcrumbs
1 egg, beaten lightly
2 large (400g) brown onions,
   extra, sliced
12 bacon rashers, halved
6 eggs, extra
6 bread rolls
75g mesclun

Combine beef in large bowl with small brown onion, garlic, sauces, seasoning, parsley, breadcrumbs and egg; shape mixture into 6 patties. *[Can be made ahead to this stage. Cover, refrigerate overnight or freeze.]*

Cook patties on heated oiled barbecue until browned both sides and cooked through. Meanwhile, cook extra onion, bacon and extra eggs on heated oiled barbecue until onion is soft, bacon crisp and eggs cooked as desired. Split rolls; toast. Sandwich mesclun, burgers, onion, bacon and eggs between roll halves.

MAKES 6

Below, from left Mega beef burgers;
Burgers bellissimo

BALSAMIC AND GINGER BEEF

¹/₂ cup (125ml) olive oil
¹/₄ cup (60ml) balsamic vinegar
1 tablespoon grated fresh ginger
1 teaspoon brown sugar
1 teaspoon soy sauce
**4 (2kg) thick T-bone steaks,
    with fillet in**

Combine oil, vinegar, ginger, sugar and sauce in jar; shake well. Reserve ¹/₄ cup (60ml) of the vinegar mixture; brush steaks all over using about half of the rest of the mixture. *[Best made ahead to this stage. Cover, refrigerate for 3 hours or overnight.]*

Cook beef on heated oiled barbecue until browned both sides. Cook in covered barbecue, using indirect heat, following manufacturer's instructions, for about 30 minutes or until cooked as desired, brushing beef occasionally with what remains of the brushing mixture. Remove beef from heat, cover; stand for about 10 minutes. Just before serving, pour reserved vinegar mixture over beef.

SERVES 4

Above Balsamic and ginger beef
Right Sweet chilli beef ribs

SWEET CHILLI BEEF RIBS

1.5kg beef spareribs
¹/₂ cup (125ml) sweet chilli sauce
1 tablespoon soy sauce
¹/₄ cup (60ml) rice wine
2 cloves garlic, crushed
1 teaspoon grated fresh ginger
**2 tablespoons finely chopped fresh
    coriander leaves**

Place spareribs in large shallow dish with combined sauces, wine, garlic, ginger and coriander. *[Best made ahead to this stage. Cover tightly, refrigerate 4 hours or overnight, or freeze.]*

Cook ribs in covered barbecue, using indirect heat, following manufacturer's instructions, about 30 minutes or until browned all over and cooked as desired.

SERVES 4

BEEF RIB ROAST WITH CAPSICUM CRUST

1.5kg standing rib roast
1/3 cup (80ml) olive oil
1/4 cup chopped fresh lemon thyme
2 cloves garlic, crushed
1 large (350g) red capsicum, seeded, chopped
1/2 cup (80g) pine nuts, toasted
1 clove garlic, crushed, extra

Place beef in large shallow dish with combined 1/4 cup (60ml) of the oil, 2 tablespoons of the thyme and 2 cloves crushed garlic. *[Best made ahead to this stage. Cover, refrigerate 3 hours or overnight.]*

Blend or process capsicum until almost smooth; strain, discard liquid. Return capsicum puree to blender; add pine nuts, extra garlic and remaining thyme and oil, process until smooth. *[Can be made ahead to this stage. Cover, refrigerate overnight.]*

Place beef on roasting rack or basket, or in disposable baking dish. Cook in covered barbecue, using indirect heat, following manufacturer's instructions, about 40 minutes. Spread beef with capsicum paste; cook about 20 minutes or until cooked as desired.

SERVES 4 TO 6

STANDING RIB ROAST PROVENÇAL

1.5kg standing rib roast
2 cups (500ml) dry red wine
2 tablespoons olive oil
3 cloves garlic, sliced
2 teaspoons chopped fresh thyme
2 teaspoons chopped fresh rosemary
3 medium (450g) white onions, quartered
4 bay leaves

Place beef in large shallow dish with combined wine, oil, garlic, herbs, onions and leaves. *[Best made ahead to this stage. Cover, refrigerate 3 hours or overnight.]*

Drain beef and onions over small pan; reserve marinade. Bring marinade to boil; simmer, uncovered, until reduced by half.

Cook beef on heated oiled barbecue until browned all over. Place beef and onions on roasting rack or basket, or in disposable baking dish. Cook in covered barbecue, using indirect heat, following manufacturer's instructions, and brushing occasionally with marinade, about 1 hour or until cooked as desired.

SERVES 4 TO 6

From left Standing rib roast provençal; Beef rib roast with capsicum crust

China and napery from Bed, Bath 'n' Table

BRAISED VINEGARED BEEF WITH CHINESE GREENS

800g rump steak, sliced thinly
1 tablespoon lime juice
1 tablespoon grated fresh ginger
2 cloves garlic, crushed
1 tablespoon finely shredded fresh
**   basil leaves**
1 teaspoon sugar
1 tablespoon vegetable oil
2 teaspoons sesame oil
1 medium (150g) white
**   onion, sliced finely**
1 small (400g) Chinese
**   cabbage, shredded**

400g bok choy, shredded
350g choy sum, shredded
2 tablespoons balsamic vinegar
250g tat soi leaves
150g snow peas
1 tablespoon sesame seeds, toasted

Combine beef in large bowl with juice, ginger, garlic, basil and sugar. *[Best made ahead to this stage. Cover, refrigerate at least 3 hours or overnight.]*

Drain beef; discard marinade. Heat half of the combined oils in wok; stir-fry onion until soft. Add beef; stir-fry, in batches, until browned and cooked as desired. Transfer beef mixture to large bowl. Add cabbage, bok choy, choy sum, half of the vinegar and remaining oils to

wok; stir-fry until just wilted, add to bowl with beef. Add tat soi, snow peas and remaining vinegar to wok; stir-fry until just wilted. Return beef and vegetables to wok; gently toss over heat until heated through, sprinkle with sesame seeds.

SERVES 4 TO 6

Above, from top Stir-fried beef with blood orange; Braised vinegared beef with Chinese greens
Right Port-smoked beef

STIR-FRIED BEEF WITH BLOOD ORANGE

You need 3 blood oranges (or substitute 4 regular oranges) for this recipe.

600g rump steak, sliced thinly
¼ cup (60ml) light olive oil
12 star anise
2 tablespoons finely grated blood orange rind
½ cup (125ml) blood orange juice
2 tablespoons peanut oil
1 medium (170g) red onion, sliced
2 cloves garlic, crushed
1 tablespoon grated fresh ginger
4 baby (600g) bok choy, sliced
½ cup (75g) dried currants
2 blood oranges, segmented
2 tablespoons soy sauce
2 tablespoons oyster sauce

Place beef in medium bowl with olive oil, star anise, rind and half of the juice. *[Best made ahead to this stage. Cover, refrigerate 6 hours or overnight.]*

Drain beef; discard marinade. Heat half the peanut oil in wok or large pan; stir-fry beef, in batches, until browned and almost cooked. Heat remaining oil in wok; stir-fry onion, garlic and ginger until soft. Add bok choy and currants; stir-fry until bok choy is just wilted. Return beef to wok, add orange segments, remaining juice and combined sauces; stir-fry about 1 minute or until beef is hot and sauce slightly thickened.

SERVES 4

PORT-SMOKED BEEF

You need 250g smoking chips for this recipe.

1.5kg beef fillet
2 tablespoons olive oil
2 cloves garlic, crushed
¼ cup (60ml) port
2 tablespoons chopped fresh oregano
1 cup (250ml) port, extra

Place beef in large bowl with combined oil, garlic, port and oregano. *[Best made ahead to this stage. Cover, refrigerate for 6 hours or overnight.]*

Combine smoking chips and extra port in small bowl; stand 2 hours. Cook beef on heated oiled barbecue just until browned all over; place beef in disposable baking dish. Place drained smoking chips in smoke box; place beside beef on barbecue. Cook in covered barbecue, using indirect heat, following manufacturer's instructions, 1 hour 30 minutes or until cooked as desired.

SERVES 4 TO 6

SUGAR AND ROSEMARY SMOKED RUMP

You need 300g heatbeads for this recipe.

25 sprigs (20g) fresh rosemary
2/3 cup (150g) white sugar
1.2kg beef rump roast

Place 300g heatbeads in large disposable baking dish; light heatbeads according to manufacturer's instructions. When flame subsides and heatbeads are coated with ash, sprinkle over rosemary and sugar. Place beef on wire cake rack; place rack over heatbeads. Cover beef loosely with foil and cook in covered barbecue, using indirect heat, following manufacturer's instructions, about 40 minutes or until cooked as desired.

SERVES 4 TO 6

THAI BEEF SALAD

500g beef rump steak
2 (260g) Lebanese cucumbers
5 large (450g) egg tomatoes
2 cups (160g) bean
  sprouts, trimmed
1 tablespoon small fresh
  mint leaves

THAI DRESSING

1/4 cup (60ml) sweet chilli sauce
1 tablespoon fish sauce
1 tablespoon lime juice
1 clove garlic, crushed
2 tablespoons chopped fresh
  coriander leaves
1 tablespoon chopped fresh
  mint leaves

Brush beef with 1/4 cup (60ml) of the Thai Dressing. *[Best made ahead to this stage. Cover, refrigerate 3 hours or overnight.]*

Cook beef on heated oiled barbecue until browned both sides and cooked as desired. Remove from heat, cover; stand for 10 minutes before slicing thinly. Meanwhile, halve cucumbers lengthways, scoop out and discard seeds; slice thinly. Cut tomatoes in quarters lengthways, remove and discard seeds; slice thinly. Just before serving, toss beef in medium bowl with cucumber, tomato, sprouts and remaining Dressing; sprinkle with small unchopped mint leaves.

Thai Dressing Combine all ingredients in jar; shake well. *[Can be made a few hours ahead. Cover tightly, refrigerate.]*

SERVES 4

Left Sugar and rosemary smoked rump
Above Thai beef salad

Poultry

Barbecuing elevates this already versatile meat to the realm of the inspired. When that quality of adaptability possessed naturally by chicken and other poultry comes into contact with a sizzling grill or hotplate, great food happens. Poultry is ready to eat if, when pierced, its juices run clear, but because this succulent meat can quickly become overcooked, bird-watching must be a part of the barbecuing process.

DRUMSTICKS WITH CRUNCHY SATAY SAUCE

8 (1.2kg) chicken drumsticks
1 tablespoon grated fresh ginger
1 clove garlic, crushed
1 cup (250ml) coconut milk
2 tablespoons lime juice
2 tablespoons soy sauce
1 tablespoon honey
1 cup (150g) finely chopped unsalted roasted peanuts
1 teaspoon Madras curry powder
1 tablespoon ground coriander

Make 2 deep cuts in thickest part of each drumstick. Combine remaining ingredients in large shallow dish; add drumsticks, turning to coat all over with marinade. *[Best made ahead to this stage. Cover, refrigerate 3 hours or overnight.]*

Drain drumsticks over medium pan; reserve marinade. Cook drumsticks on heated oiled barbecue until browned all over. Cook in covered barbecue, using indirect heat, following manufacturer's instructions, about 15 minutes or until browned all over and tender.

Meanwhile, place reserved marinade on barbecue. Bring to boil; simmer, stirring, about 5 minutes or until thick. Serve satay sauce with drumsticks.

SERVES 4

STICKY BBQ CHICKEN

8 (1.3kg) chicken thigh cutlets, on bone
2 tablespoons honey
1 clove garlic, crushed
1 teaspoon grated fresh ginger
1 tablespoon soy sauce
1 tablespoon sweet chilli sauce

Place chicken in large shallow dish with combined honey, garlic, ginger and sauces. *[Best made ahead to this stage. Cover, refrigerate 3 hours or overnight.]*

Drain chicken over small bowl; reserve marinade. Place chicken on oiled roasting rack or basket, or in disposable baking dish, brush with reserved marinade. Cook chicken in covered barbecue, using indirect heat, following manufacturer's instructions, about 30 minutes or until browned both sides and tender. Turn chicken after 15 minutes; brush with marinade.

SERVES 4

From left Drumsticks with crunchy satay sauce; Sticky bbq chicken

TANDOORI CHICKEN WITH CUCUMBER MINT RAITA

You need 250g smoking chips for this recipe.

1/2 cup (135g) tandoori paste
1 cup (250ml) yogurt
2 cloves garlic, crushed
2 teaspoons grated fresh ginger
1.6kg chicken
1 cup (250ml) green ginger wine

CUCUMBER MINT RAITA
1 (130g) Lebanese cucumber
1 cup (250ml) yogurt
2 tablespoons finely chopped fresh
    mint leaves
1/2 teaspoon ground cumin
1/2 teaspoon ground coriander

Combine paste, yogurt, garlic and ginger in large bowl, add chicken; using hands, rub tandoori mixture all over chicken. *[Best made ahead to this stage. Cover, refrigerate overnight or freeze.]*

Combine smoking chips and wine in small bowl; stand 2 hours. Tuck chicken wings under body, tie legs together with kitchen string; place chicken on oiled roasting rack. Place drained smoking chips in smoke box; place alongside chicken on barbecue. Cook in covered barbecue, using indirect heat, following manufacturer's instructions, about 1 hour and 20 minutes or until browned all over and tender. Serve with Cucumber Mint Raita.

Cucumber Mint Raita Peel cucumber; halve lengthways, discard seeds. Chop cucumber coarsely; combine in small bowl with remaining ingredients. Cover, refrigerate. *[Best made no more than 3 hours ahead of serving.]*

SERVES 4 TO 6

Left Tandoori chicken with cucumber mint raita
Above Turkey with raisin and Brazil
nut seasoning

TURKEY WITH RAISIN AND BRAZIL NUT SEASONING

20g butter
1 medium (150g) onion, chopped
1 1/4 cups (185g) Brazil
    nuts, chopped
1 1/2 cups (250g) raisins, chopped
3.5kg turkey
2 tablespoons soy sauce
1 tablespoon honey

Heat butter in medium pan; cook onion, stirring, until soft. Remove from heat, stir in nuts and raisins.

Discard turkey neck and giblets. Rinse turkey under cold water; pat dry inside and out. Tuck wings under body; spoon raisin seasoning into body cavity. Tuck trimmed neck flap under body, securing with toothpicks; tie legs together with kitchen string. Place turkey on roasting rack or basket, or in disposable baking dish. Brush with combined sauce and honey. Cook in covered barbecue, using indirect heat, following manufacturer's instructions, 2 1/2 hours or until browned all over and tender.

SERVES 6 TO 8

CHICKEN WITH CARAMELISED PEAR

**4 (680g) single chicken
    breast fillets**
40g butter
**1/4 cup (50g) firmly packed
    brown sugar**
**3 large (990g) pears, peeled,
    sliced thickly**
12 slices (180g) prosciutto

Cut each chicken fillet in 3 strips diagonally; place each strip between pieces of plastic wrap, pound gently with meat mallet until just flattened.

Melt butter and sugar in medium pan on barbecue; cook pear, stirring, until pear caramelises and sauce thickens. Meanwhile, cook chicken strips on heated oiled barbecue until browned both sides and tender. Cook prosciutto on heated oiled barbecue until browned both sides and crisp. Serve chicken with prosciutto and caramelised pear.

SERVES 4

ROSEMARY-SMOKED CHICKEN BREAST

You need 250g smoking chips for this recipe.

1 clove garlic, crushed
1 1/2 cups (375ml) dry white wine
**1 tablespoon finely chopped
    fresh rosemary**
**4 (680g) single chicken
    breast fillets**
2 cups (500ml) water
1 clove garlic, crushed, extra
**2 tablespoons coarsely chopped
    fresh rosemary, extra**
2 tablespoons olive oil
200g oyster mushrooms
200g enoki mushrooms
400g baby spinach leaves

Combine garlic, 1/2 cup of the wine and finely chopped rosemary in large shallow dish; add chicken, mix well. *[Must be made ahead to this stage. Cover, refrigerate for 3 hours or overnight.]*

Combine water, remaining wine, extra garlic and extra rosemary in large bowl; add smoking chips, mix well. Stand at least 2 hours or overnight.

Cook chicken both sides on heated oiled barbecue 2 minutes each side. Place chicken on oiled roasting rack or basket, or in disposable baking dish. Place drained smoking chips in smoke box; place alongside chicken on barbecue. Cook in covered barbecue, using indirect heat, following manufacturer's instructions, about 35 minutes or until browned all over and tender.

Just before serving, heat half the oil in wok; stir-fry oyster mushrooms about 3 minutes or until just tender, remove from wok. Heat remaining oil in wok; stir-fry enoki mushrooms and spinach only long enough to heat, not wilt. Serve chicken with spinach and mushrooms.

SERVES 4

Right Rosemary-smoked chicken breast
Above Chicken with caramelised pear

Setting from Accoutrement

PORTUGUESE-STYLE SEARED SPATCHCOCK

4 (2kg) spatchcocks
1 tablespoon cracked black pepper
1 tablespoon ground cumin
1 tablespoon lemon juice
1 tablespoon olive oil
1/2 teaspoon chilli powder
1/2 teaspoon hot paprika
1/4 teaspoon cayenne pepper
1 clove garlic, crushed

Cut along both sides of each spatchcock backbone; discard backbones.

Insert metal skewer through thigh and opposite wing. Repeat with other thigh and wing.

Combine remaining ingredients in small bowl; mix to a smooth paste. Using hands, rub chilli paste all over spatchcock pieces. Cook in covered barbecue, using indirect heat, following manufacturer's instructions, 20 minutes. Turn spatchcock; cook about 20 minutes or until browned all over and tender.

SERVES 4

SPATCHCOCK WITH FENNEL

2 (1kg) spatchcocks
40g butter
1 medium (500g) fennel bulb, sliced
1/4 cup (60ml) Pernod

Cut along both sides of each spatchcock backbone; discard backbones. Place spatchcock, breast side up, on board; press breastbone to flatten spatchcock.

Heat butter in large pan; cook fennel, stirring, until soft and browned lightly; add Pernod. Transfer onion mixture to disposable baking dish. Cook spatchcock on heated oiled barbecue until browned both sides; place spatchcock on top of fennel mixture in dish. Cook spatchcock in covered barbecue, using indirect heat, following manufacturer's instructions, about 30 minutes or until browned all over and tender.

SERVES 2

Knife and fork from Accoutrement; basket, bowl and plate from Shack

ROASTED WHOLE CHICKEN WITH CARAMELISED LEMON

40g butter
2 medium (280g) lemons, sliced
4 small (400g) red onions, chopped
1.6kg chicken
1/4 cup (60ml) olive oil
1/4 cup (60ml) lemon juice

Heat half the butter in medium pan; cook lemon, stirring, until just softened and caramelised slightly. Remove from pan; cool. Heat remaining butter in same pan; cook onion, stirring, until soft and browned lightly. Remove from pan; cool.

Push lemon between flesh and skin of chicken; spoon onion into body cavity. Tuck trimmed neck flap under body,

securing with toothpicks; tie legs together with kitchen string. Place chicken on oiled roasting rack or basket, or in disposable baking dish. Brush all over with combined oil and juice. Cook chicken in covered barbecue, using indirect heat, following manufacturer's instructions, about 1 hour and 20 minutes or until browned all over and tender.

SERVES 4

Right, from top Portuguese-style seared spatchcock; Spatchcock with fennel
Above Roasted whole chicken with caramelised lemon

Setting from Wednesday's Value Homewares

APRICOT-SEASONED CHICKEN

30g butter
3 large (600g) brown
   onions, chopped
250g minced chicken
1/4 cup (35g) chopped
   dried apricots
1 cup (70g) stale breadcrumbs
2 tablespoons cream
1.4kg boned chicken
1 tablespoon olive oil
2 cups (500ml) apricot nectar

Heat butter in small pan; cook about a third of the onion, stirring, until just soft. Combine cooled onion in large bowl with the minced chicken, apricots, breadcrumbs and cream.

Open chicken out on flat surface, skin-side down; mound apricot filling mixture in centre of chicken.

Roll chicken tightly; tie with kitchen string at 2cm intervals. Place in oiled disposable baking dish. Cook in covered barbecue, using indirect heat, following manufacturer's instructions, for about 1 1/2 hours or until browned all over and tender. Remove chicken from dish, keep warm; reserve pan juices.

Heat oil in medium pan on barbecue; cook remaining onion, stirring, until browned. Add nectar and pan juices, bring to boil; simmer, uncovered, 5 minutes. Serve apricot sauce with chicken.

SERVES 4 TO 6

GRILLED SPATCHCOCK WITH CITRUS FLAVOURS

4 (2kg) spatchcocks
1/4 cup (60ml) marmalade
1 tablespoon finely grated
   lemon rind
1 tablespoon finely grated lime rind
1 tablespoon lemon juice
1 tablespoon lime juice
1 tablespoon Grand Marnier
1 tablespoon chopped fresh oregano
1 tablespoon cracked black pepper
2 tablespoons olive oil

Cut along both sides of each spatchcock backbone; discard backbones. Cut each spatchcock in half between breasts. Combine remaining ingredients in large bowl; add spatchcock pieces, mix well. *[Best made ahead to this stage. Cover, refrigerate 3 hours or overnight.]*

Place spatchcock on heated oiled barbecue. Cover, cook, using indirect heat, following manufacturer's instructions, 20 minutes. Turn spatchcock, cook 20 minutes or until browned both sides and tender.

SERVES 4

HOT HOT HOT
CHICKEN WINGS

12 (1.5kg) chicken wings
3/4 cup (180ml) vegetable oil
2 cloves garlic, crushed
1 tablespoon hot paprika
1 tablespoon ground cumin
1 tablespoon ground turmeric
1 tablespoon ground coriander
1 tablespoon grated lime rind
2 teaspoons chilli powder
2 teaspoons hot curry powder

Make 2 deep cuts in thickest part of each wing. Combine remaining ingredients in large bowl; add chicken wings, mix well. *[Must be made ahead to this stage. Cover, refrigerate 3 hours or overnight.]*

Cook wings on heated oiled barbecue, uncovered, until they are browned both sides and tender.

SERVES 4

Left Apricot-seasoned chicken
Above, from top Grilled spatchcock with citrus flavours; Hot hot hot chicken wings

Platters, glasses and salad servers from Opus

VODKA AND SICHUAN PEPPER GLAZED CHICKEN

1/2 cup (110g) sugar
1/2 cup (125ml) lemon juice
1/4 cup (60ml) vodka
1 tablespoon water
1 teaspoon roasted crushed
   Sichuan peppercorns
1.6kg chicken

BLINI
3 large (900g) potatoes
2 tablespoons peanut oil
2 small (160g) white onions,
   chopped finely
3 cloves garlic, crushed
1 1/2 cups (225g) self-raising flour
2 teaspoons sugar
2 eggs, beaten lightly
1 1/2 cups (375ml) milk

Barbecue from Kangaroo TentCity & BBQ's

LIME CHICKEN ON LEMON GRASS SKEWERS

6 x 30cm-long fresh lemon
   grass stalks
1/3 cup (80ml) peanut oil
1 tablespoon grated lime rind
1/4 cup coarsely chopped fresh
   coriander leaves
6 single (1.2kg) chicken
   breast fillets
1/4 cup (60ml) lime juice
2 small bird's-eye chillies, seeded,
   chopped finely
1/3 cup (80ml) macadamia oil
1 tablespoon raw sugar
1 clove garlic, crushed

Cut 3cm off the end of each lemon grass stalk; reserve stalks. Chop the 3cm pieces finely then combine in large shallow dish with peanut oil, rind and coriander.

Cut each fillet in 4 strips crossways; thread 4 strips on each lemon grass stalk "skewer". Place skewers in dish, turning to coat chicken in lemon grass marinade. *[Must be made ahead to this stage. Cover, refrigerate 3 hours or overnight.]*

Cook skewers on heated oiled barbecue, uncovered, until chicken is browned all over and tender. Meanwhile, combine remaining ingredients in jar, shake well; serve with chicken skewers.

SERVES 6

Combine sugar, juice, vodka, water and pepper in small pan. Boil, uncovered, for about 5 minutes or until slightly thickened; divide glaze into two portions. Place chicken on roasting rack or basket. Cook in covered barbecue, using indirect heat, following manufacturer's instructions, 1 hour. Brush chicken with one portion of glaze, cook 20 minutes more or until chicken is browned all over and tender. Just before serving, brush with remaining glaze. Serve chicken with blini.

Blini Boil, steam or microwave potatoes until tender; drain, mash. Heat oil in large pan, add onion and garlic; cook, stirring, until onion is soft. Combine mashed potato and onion mixture in large bowl with flour, sugar, eggs and milk. Cook 1/4 cup measures of potato mixture on heated oiled barbecue plate until browned both sides and cooked through.

SERVES 4 TO 6

MARMALADE CHICKEN WITH ASPARAGUS WALNUT SALAD

1 cup (350g) orange marmalade
1/4 cup (60ml) Grand Marnier
1/4 cup (60ml) orange juice
1.6kg chicken

ASPARAGUS WALNUT SALAD
500g asparagus
1/4 cup (30g) finely chopped walnuts, toasted
2 teaspoons seeded mustard
1 tablespoon red wine vinegar
1 small shallot, chopped finely
1/4 cup (60ml) extra virgin olive oil
100g baby rocket leaves

Combine marmalade, liqueur and juice in small pan. Bring to boil, simmer, uncovered, for about 5 minutes or until glaze thickens. Divide glaze into two portions. Place chicken on roasting rack or basket.

Cook in covered barbecue, using indirect heat, following manufacturer's instructions, 1 hour. Brush chicken with one portion of glaze, cook 20 minutes more or until browned all over and tender. Just before serving, brush with remaining glaze. Serve chicken with Asparagus Walnut Salad.

Asparagus Walnut Salad Cut asparagus spears into 10cm lengths. Boil, steam or microwave asparagus until tender. Blend or process half the walnuts with mustard, vinegar, shallot and oil until smooth. Just before serving, combine asparagus with rocket and walnut dressing, sprinkle with remaining walnuts.

SERVES 4 TO 6

Left Lime chicken on lemon grass skewers
Below, from left Marmalade chicken with asparagus walnut salad; Vodka and Sichuan pepper glazed chicken

MARJORAM AND ORANGE TURKEY

You need 3 small oranges for this recipe.

4kg turkey
2 small (360g) oranges, quartered
6 fresh bay leaves
2 sprigs fresh marjoram

ORANGE BUTTER

¼ cup (60ml) dry white wine
2 teaspoons finely grated orange rind
100g butter, chopped
1 clove garlic, crushed
2 tablespoons brown sugar
2 tablespoons orange juice

Discard turkey neck and giblets. Rinse turkey under cold water; pat dry inside and out. Tuck wings under body; place oranges, bay leaves and marjoram loosely inside body cavity. Tuck trimmed neck flap under body, securing with toothpicks; tie legs together with kitchen string. Place turkey on oiled roasting rack or basket, or in disposable baking dish, brush with Orange Butter. Cook in covered barbecue, using indirect heat, following manufacturer's instructions, about 2½ hours or until browned all over and tender; brush occasionally with Orange Butter, cover wings with foil if overbrowning.

Orange Butter Combine all ingredients in small pan; cook, stirring, until combined and heated through.

SERVES 8

REDCURRANT-GLAZED DUCK

2kg duck
2 teaspoons olive oil
1 medium (150g) onion, chopped
2 tablespoons brown sugar
2 tablespoons red wine vinegar
⅓ cup (80ml) orange juice
⅓ cup (80ml) chicken stock
2 tablespoons redcurrant jelly
2 tablespoons flaked almonds, toasted

Place duck in disposable baking dish; cook in covered barbecue, using indirect heat, following manufacturer's instructions, 1 hour. Remove duck; using scissors, cut into 8 pieces. Discard fat then return duck pieces to dish.

Heat oil in small pan on barbecue; cook onion, stirring, until soft. Add sugar and vinegar; cook, stirring, until vinegar has almost evaporated. Add juice, stock and jelly to pan; cook, stirring, until jelly melts and mixture thickens slightly. Pour glaze over duck in dish, return to covered barbecue; cook about 30 minutes or until duck is browned all over and tender. Serve sprinkled with toasted flaked almonds.

SERVES 4

Below Marjoram and orange turkey
Right, from top Duck with Madeira and juniper berries; Redcurrant-glazed duck

Barbecue from Barbeques Galore

DUCK WITH MADEIRA AND JUNIPER BERRIES

2 teaspoons dried juniper berries
1 tablespoon Sichuan pepper
6 star anise
2 teaspoons salt
2kg duck
2/3 cup (160ml) Madeira

Crush or process berries, pepper, star anise and salt until powdered. Place duck in disposable baking dish, tuck wings under body, securing with toothpicks; tie legs together with kitchen string. Combine crushed juniper berry mixture with Madeira in small jug; pour over duck. *[Best made ahead to this stage. Cover, refrigerate 3 hours or overnight.]*

Cook duck in covered barbecue, using indirect heat, following manufacturer's instructions, about 1 hour and 40 minutes or until browned all over and tender; brush occasionally with pan juices.

SERVES 4

Glasses from Wednesdays Value Homewares; plates and platter from Country Floors

QUAIL WITH PANCETTA AND SUN-DRIED CAPSICUM

2/3 cup (160ml) peanut oil
2 tablespoons balsamic vinegar
2 tablespoons lemon juice
2 tablespoons soy sauce
1 tablespoon brown sugar
6 quail
12 slices (180g) pancetta
1 cup (200g) sun-dried capsicums
  in oil, drained

Combine oil, vinegar, juice, sauce and sugar in large bowl; add quail, mix well. *[Must be made ahead to this stage. Cover, refrigerate 3 hours or overnight.]*

Drain quail over small pan; reserve marinade. Tie legs together with kitchen string; place quail in oiled roasting basket or disposable baking dish. Cook in covered barbecue, using indirect heat, following manufacturer's instructions, for 30 minutes or until browned and tender.

Meanwhile, cook pancetta on heated oiled barbecue until browned and crisp.

Place reserved marinade on barbecue, bring to boil; simmer, whisking, 2 minutes. Serve quail with capsicum, pancetta and hot marinade.

SERVES 4

QUAIL GRILLED NORTH-AFRICAN STYLE

1/2 cup (100g) couscous
1/2 cup (125ml) boiling water
1 tablespoon olive oil
1 small (80g) white onion, finely chopped
2 cloves garlic, crushed
2 teaspoons ground cumin
2 teaspoons ground coriander
2 green onions, chopped
1/4 cup (35g) dried currants
1/4 cup (35g) dried apricots, sliced
2 tablespoons finely chopped fresh coriander leaves
2 tablespoons finely chopped fresh mint leaves
12 quail

CUMIN DRESSING

2 tablespoons olive oil
1 tablespoon lemon juice
1 teaspoon cumin seeds
1 clove garlic, crushed
1/4 teaspoon sugar

Combine couscous and the boiling water in medium heatproof bowl; cover, stand for about 5 minutes or until water is absorbed.

Meanwhile, heat oil in large pan; cook white onion, garlic and spices, stirring, until onion is soft. Using a fork, toss couscous, green onion, fruit and herbs into spice mixture. *[Can be made ahead to this stage. Cover, refrigerate overnight.]*

Rinse quail under cold water; pat dry inside and out. Tuck wings under body, securing with toothpicks. Spoon couscous mixture into body cavity, securing opening with toothpicks. Secure legs with kitchen string; place quail directly on oiled grill or plate. Cook in covered barbecue, using indirect heat, following manufacturer's instructions, for about 20 minutes or until browned all over and tender. Drizzle with Cumin Dressing.

Cumin Dressing Whisk all ingredients together in small bowl.

SERVES 4 TO 6

LIME AND GREEN PEPPERCORN BBQUAIL

12 quail
1/2 cup (125ml) olive oil
1/4 cup (45g) drained green peppercorns, crushed
2 tablespoons finely grated lime rind
1/2 cup (125ml) lime juice
2 cloves garlic, crushed
2 tablespoons finely chopped fresh coriander leaves

Plate, cutlery and tea-towel from Accoutrement

Cut along both sides of each quail backbone; discard backbones. Cut each quail in half along breastbone. Combine remaining ingredients in large bowl; add quail pieces, mix well. *[Best made ahead to this stage. Cover, refrigerate for 3 hours or overnight.]*

Drain quail over small bowl; reserve marinade. Cook quail on heated oiled barbecue, brushing frequently with reserved marinade, about 5 minutes each side or until browned all over and tender.

SERVES 4 TO 6

CHICKEN TIKKA WITH GRILLED BANANAS

1/3 cup (80g) tikka curry paste
1/2 cup (125ml) yogurt
2 cloves garlic, crushed
2 teaspoons grated fresh ginger
1 tablespoon chopped fresh coriander leaves
1 teaspoon ground coriander
1 teaspoon ground cumin
1.6kg chicken

GRILLED BANANAS

4 medium (800g) bananas
1 bird's-eye chilli, chopped finely
1 teaspoon finely grated lime rind
1/2 cup (125ml) coconut cream

Combine paste, yogurt, garlic, ginger, fresh and ground coriander, and cumin in large bowl. Add chicken; using hands, rub tikka mixture all over chicken. *[Must be made ahead. Cover, refrigerate overnight.]*

Place chicken on oiled roasting rack or basket, or in disposable baking dish. Cook in covered barbecue, using indirect heat, following manufacturer's instructions, about 1 hour and 20 minutes or until browned all over and tender. Serve with Grilled Bananas.

Grilled Bananas Cut unpeeled bananas in half lengthways; cut each half into 2 pieces. Combine chilli, rind and cream in small bowl. Brush a little of the mixture over cut side of each banana. Cook banana on heated oiled barbecue until browned and soft. Drizzle banana with remaining cream mixture, if desired.

SERVES 4 TO 6

Left, from bottom Lime and green peppercorn BBQuail; Quail grilled North-African style; Quail with pancetta and sun-dried capsicum
Above Chicken tikka with grilled bananas

Lamb

Lamb barbecues to juicy perfection, marrying happily with the flavours of many cuisines from around the world. Try lamb with black sesame seed dressing, for instance, or lamb with garlic and shiitake mushrooms. For the best results, don't overcook lamb – the meat should be moist and pink on the inside. And, for added succulence, allow larger cuts to rest in a warm place for at least 15 minutes before carving.

MINI ROAST WITH HORSERADISH CREAM

1/3 cup (80ml) redcurrant jelly
1/4 cup (60ml) olive oil
4 (800g) mini lamb roasts
5 medium (1kg) pink eye potatoes
10 cloves garlic, unpeeled
2 tablespoons sea salt flakes
1/4 cup (60ml) hazelnut oil
1/4 cup grated fresh horseradish
1 1/2 cups (375ml) creme fraiche

Combine jelly and olive oil in large bowl, add lamb; mix well. [Best made ahead to this stage. Cover, refrigerate 3 hours or overnight.]

Cut each potato into 8 wedges. Combine potato, garlic, salt and hazelnut oil in disposable baking dish. Cook in covered barbecue, using indirect heat, following manufacturer's instructions, 35 minutes.

Remove barbecue cover, cook lamb on heated oiled barbecue until browned all over. Replace cover, cook, using indirect heat, about 10 minutes or until lamb is cooked as desired.

Serve lamb and potato wedges with combined horseradish and creme fraiche.

SERVES 4

LEMON AND ARTICHOKE RACK OF LAMB

2 racks of lamb with 8 cutlets each
2 medium (300g) brown
  onions, sliced
1 medium (140g) lemon,
400g can artichoke hearts,
  drained, quartered
2 tablespoons drained capers
30g butter
1 teaspoon brown sugar

Cook lamb and onion on heated oiled barbecue plate until lamb is browned all over and onion soft. Cut lemon into 8 wedges. Place lamb, onion and lemon in disposable baking dish with remaining ingredients. Cook in covered barbecue, using indirect heat, following manufacturer's instructions, about 30 minutes or until lamb is cooked as desired.

SERVES 4

Right, from top Mini roast with horseradish cream; Lemon and artichoke rack of lamb

SUMAC LAMB ROASTS WITH CITRUS TABBOULEH

2 tablespoons sumac
2 tablespoons olive oil
1 clove garlic, crushed
4 (800g) mini lamb roasts
200ml yogurt

CITRUS TABBOULEH
1/2 cup (80g) burghul
1 cup (100g) coarsely chopped
    flat-leaf parsley leaves
6 small (780g) tomatoes, seeded,
    chopped finely
2 tablespoons coarsely chopped
    fresh mint leaves
2 tablespoons coarsely chopped
    fresh basil leaves
2 tablespoons grated lemon rind
2 tablespoons lemon juice
2 cloves garlic, crushed
1 teaspoon cracked black pepper

Combine sumac, oil and garlic in large shallow dish, add lamb; mix well. *[Best made ahead. Cover, refrigerate for 3 hours or overnight.]*

Cook lamb, uncovered, on heated oiled barbecue until browned all over and cooked as desired. Serve lamb with yogurt and Citrus Tabbouleh.

Citrus Tabbouleh Place burghul in small bowl, cover with cold water, stand 15 minutes; drain. Rinse burghul under cold water, drain; squeeze to remove excess moisture. Combine burghul in medium bowl with remaining ingredients. *[Best made just before serving.]*

SERVES 4

RED WINE LAMB WITH GARLIC SMASH POTATOES

1 cup (250ml) dry red wine
1/4 cup finely chopped
    fresh rosemary
2 cloves garlic, crushed
2kg leg of lamb
1/4 cup (60ml) seeded mustard
1/4 cup finely chopped fresh
    mint leaves

GARLIC SMASH POTATOES
8 medium (1.6kg) potatoes
2 cloves garlic, crushed
100g butter, melted

Combine wine, rosemary and garlic in large shallow dish, add lamb. *[Best made ahead. Cover, refrigerate for 3 hours or overnight.]*

Drain lamb; discard marinade. Place lamb on roasting rack or basket, or in disposable baking dish. Cook in covered barbecue, using indirect heat, following

GARLIC AND ROSEMARY SMOKED LAMB

You need 250g smoking chips for this recipe.

1kg boned, rolled lamb loin
4 cloves garlic, halved
8 fresh rosemary sprigs
1 teaspoon dried chilli flakes
1 tablespoon olive oil

Place lamb in large bowl. Pierce lamb in 8 places with sharp knife; push garlic halves and rosemary sprigs into cuts. Sprinkle lamb with chilli; rub with oil. *[Best made ahead. Cover, refrigerate for 3 hours or overnight.]*

Soak smoking chips in large bowl of water 2 hours.

Cook lamb, uncovered, on heated oiled barbecue until browned all over. Place drained chips in smoke box on barbecue next to lamb. Cook lamb in covered barbecue, using indirect heat, following manufacturer's instructions, for about 40 minutes or until cooked as desired.

SERVES 4 TO 6

manufacturer's instructions, 1 hour. Spread lamb with mustard, sprinkle with mint; cook, covered, about 15 minutes or until cooked as desired. Serve lamb with Garlic Smash Potatoes.

Garlic Smash Potatoes Wrap potatoes individually in foil; cook in covered barbecue, using indirect heat, following manufacturer's instructions, about 45 minutes or until tender. Place potatoes on flat surface; hit with a meat mallet to flatten. Just before serving, remove foil; brush potatoes with combined garlic and butter.

SERVES 4 TO 6

Left Garlic and rosemary smoked lamb
Above Sumac lamb roasts with citrus tabbouleh
Right Red wine lamb with garlic smash potatoes

MINTED LAMB WITH BABY BEETROOT AND ROCKET SALAD

1/4 cup (60ml) olive oil
2 cloves garlic, crushed
1/2 cup chopped fresh mint leaves
2 racks of lamb with 8 cutlets each
1 tablespoon olive oil, extra
1/4 cup chopped fresh mint leaves, extra

BABY BEETROOT AND ROCKET SALAD
1kg bunch baby beetroot
1 medium (140g) lemon
250g rocket
2 tablespoons olive oil
2 tablespoons raspberry vinegar
1/4 cup (20g) parmesan cheese flakes

Combine oil, garlic and mint in large shallow dish; add lamb, mix well. [Best made ahead. Cover, refrigerate for 3 hours or overnight.]

Drain lamb; discard marinade. Place lamb on roasting rack or basket, or in disposable baking dish. Cook in covered barbecue, using indirect heat, following manufacturer's instructions, 25 minutes.

Brush top of lamb with extra oil, sprinkle with extra mint; cook, covered, about 10 minutes or until cooked as desired. Remove from heat, cover; stand 10 minutes before serving with Baby Beetroot and Rocket Salad.

Baby Beetroot and Rocket Salad Cut beetroot stems 3cm from top of beetroot; remove and discard roots. Wrap beetroot in foil, cook next to lamb on heated barbecue 10 minutes or until tender; remove from foil. Remove skin from beetroot. Peel rind thinly from lemon, avoiding any white pith; cut rind into thin strips. Place rocket and beetroot in medium bowl, drizzle with combined oil and vinegar, sprinkle with lemon rind. Scatter parmesan over salad.

SERVES 4

LAMB WITH GARLIC AND SHIITAKE MUSHROOMS

12 cloves garlic, peeled
1 tablespoon sugar
¼ cup (60ml) olive oil
3 (900g) lamb eye of loin
400g shiitake mushrooms, halved
40g butter, melted
2 tablespoons chopped fresh chives

Combine garlic, sugar and 2 tablespoons of the oil in disposable baking dish. Cook in covered barbecue, using indirect heat, following manufacturer's instructions, about 15 minutes or until garlic is soft and slightly caramelised. Remove from barbecue; cover to keep warm.

Brush lamb with remaining oil; cook, uncovered, on heated oiled barbecue until browned all over and cooked as desired.

Meanwhile, toss mushrooms, butter and chives together in large bowl. Transfer mushroom mixture to heated oiled barbecue plate; cook until tender. Serve lamb with roasted garlic and mushrooms.

SERVES 4 TO 6

Above, from top Minted lamb with baby beetroot and rocket salad; Lamb with garlic and shiitake mushrooms

MUSTARD LAMB CUTLETS WITH BASIL CREAM

2 racks of lamb with 8 cutlets each
1/2 cup (125ml) olive oil
1/2 cup coarsely chopped fresh basil leaves
1 clove garlic, crushed
1kg kipfler potatoes
1 tablespoon olive oil, extra
2 tablespoons seeded mustard

BASIL CREAM

2 teaspoons olive oil
1 medium (150g) white onion, sliced finely
1 clove garlic, crushed
1/2 cup (125ml) dry white wine
300ml cream
1/2 cup coarsely chopped fresh basil leaves

Cut lamb racks into double cutlets. Combine oil, basil and garlic in large shallow dish, add cutlets; mix well. *[Best made ahead. Cover, refrigerate 3 hours or overnight.]*

Cut potatoes in half lengthways, brush with extra oil; place in disposable baking dish. Cook in covered barbecue, using indirect heat, following manufacturer's instructions, about 45 minutes or until potatoes are softened; keep warm.

Drain cutlets; discard marinade. Cook cutlets, uncovered, on heated oiled barbecue until browned all over and cooked as desired. Spread with mustard, serve with Basil Cream and potatoes.

Basil Cream Heat oil in medium pan on barbecue, cook onion and garlic, stirring, until soft. Add wine, simmer, uncovered, 5 minutes or until reduced by half. Add cream; boil 5 minutes or until sauce thickens. Remove from heat, stir in basil; serve immediately.

SERVES 4 TO 6

LAMB AND ARTICHOKE KEBABS

Soak bamboo skewers in water for about 1 hour to prevent them scorching.

1kg diced lamb
2 x 400g cans artichoke hearts, drained, halved
1 large (350g) red capsicum, chopped
300g button mushrooms, halved

GARLIC BASIL DRESSING

1/2 cup (125ml) red wine vinegar
1/4 cup (60ml) olive oil
1 tablespoon shredded fresh basil leaves
1 clove garlic, crushed
1 teaspoon sugar
1 teaspoon Dijon mustard

Thread lamb, artichoke hearts, capsicum and mushrooms on 8 large skewers. [Can be made a day ahead to this stage. Cover, refrigerate overnight.]

Cook kebabs, in batches, on heated oiled barbecue until browned all over and cooked as desired.

Serve with Garlic Basil Dressing.

Garlic Basil Dressing Combine all ingredients in jar; shake well.

SERVES 4

MINTED BUTTERFLIED LEG OF LAMB

1.5kg butterflied leg of lamb
1 cup (250ml) dry white wine
3 cloves garlic, crushed
1/4 cup chopped fresh mint leaves
1/4 cup chopped fresh parsley
2 tablespoons soy sauce
1 tablespoon brown sugar

Combine lamb with remaining ingredients in disposable baking dish. [Best made ahead. Cover, refrigerate overnight.]

Cook lamb in covered barbecue, using indirect heat, following manufacturer's instructions, about 50 minutes or until cooked as desired. During cooking, brush lamb occasionally with pan juices.

SERVES 4 TO 6

Above, from top Lamb and artichoke kebabs; Minted butterflied leg of lamb
Left Mustard lamb cutlets with basil cream

MINT AND LIME LAMB WITH SALSA

1/2 cup (125ml) olive oil
2 cloves garlic, crushed
2 teaspoons grated lime rind
2 tablespoons lime juice
2 tablespoons chopped fresh
 mint leaves
8 lamb chops

WATERMELON AND MANGO SALSA
1kg chopped watermelon
3 small (900g) mangoes, chopped
2 bird's-eye chillies,
 seeded, chopped
1/4 cup shredded fresh
 coriander leaves
2 tablespoons grated lime rind
1/4 cup (60ml) raspberry vinegar

Combine oil, garlic, rind, juice and mint in medium bowl, add chops; mix well. *[Best made ahead to this stage. Cover, refrigerate 3 hours or overnight.]*

Cook chops, uncovered, on heated oiled barbecue until browned both sides and cooked as desired. Serve with Watermelon and Mango Salsa.

Watermelon and Mango Salsa Combine all ingredients in large bowl; cover, refrigerate 3 hours.

SERVES 4

Above Mint and lime lamb with salsa
Right, clockwise from top Beetroot and yogurt dip; Minted pesto; Indian chutney; Raita; Red onion and balsamic jam

Serve these accompaniments with perfectly barbecued chops or cutlets

RAITA

200ml yogurt
1/2 (65g) Lebanese cucumber, seeded, chopped finely
1 teaspoon cumin seeds, toasted
1 clove garlic, crushed
1 tablespoon lemon juice

Combine all ingredients in small bowl.

MAKES ABOUT 1 CUP (250ml)

INDIAN CHUTNEY

1 1/2 cups (375ml) cider vinegar
3/4 cup (150g) firmly packed brown sugar
1 medium (150g) brown onion, chopped
400g can tomatoes
450g can crushed pineapple
2 cups (375g) mixed dried fruit
1 tablespoon chopped glace ginger
1 clove garlic, crushed
1 tablespoon ground cumin
1 tablespoon ground coriander
2 teaspoons ground cloves
1 cinnamon stick

Combine all ingredients in large pan. Cook, stirring, over low heat until sugar is dissolved. Bring to boil; simmer, uncovered, stirring occasionally, for about 1 hour or until thickened. Spoon into hot sterilised jars; seal.

MAKES ABOUT 3 CUPS (750ml)

MINTED PESTO

1 cup fresh mint leaves
1/2 cup (125ml) olive oil
2 tablespoons grated parmesan cheese
2 cloves garlic, crushed
2 tablespoons pine nuts, toasted

Blend or process all ingredients until smooth. Store, covered, in refrigerator.

MAKES ABOUT 3/4 CUP (180ml)

BEETROOT AND YOGURT DIP

225g can beetroot slices, drained
1/4 cup (60ml) yogurt
1 tablespoon chopped fresh coriander leaves
1 clove garlic, crushed
1 teaspoon ground cumin

Blend or process all ingredients until smooth. Store, covered, in refrigerator.

MAKES ABOUT 1 CUP (250ml)

RED ONION AND BALSAMIC JAM

1/4 cup (60ml) olive oil
3 medium (510g) red onions, sliced
1/4 cup (50g) firmly packed brown sugar
1/3 cup (80ml) balsamic vinegar
1/2 teaspoon dill seeds
1/4 cup (60ml) chicken stock

Heat oil in pan; cook onion, stirring, until soft and browned lightly. Stir in sugar, vinegar, seeds and stock. Simmer, uncovered, about 20 minutes or until mixture is thickened.

MAKES ABOUT 1 1/2 CUPS (375ml)

LAMB WITH BLACK SESAME SEED DRESSING

1/3 cup (80ml) soy sauce
1/3 cup (80ml) oyster sauce
1/3 cup (80ml) sweet chilli sauce
1/4 cup (60ml) water
3 cloves garlic, crushed
3 (900g) lamb eye of loin
1/4 cup (35g) black sesame seeds

POTATO ALMOND ROSTI

4 medium (800g) potatoes,
  grated finely
1 cup (100g) grated
  mozzarella cheese
1/2 cup (60g) almond meal
1/3 cup finely chopped chives
1/3 cup (55g) finely chopped almonds
2 tablespoons sumac

Combine sauces, water and garlic in large bowl, add lamb; mix well. *[Best made ahead to this stage. Cover, refrigerate 3 hours or overnight.]*

Drain lamb over small pan; reserve marinade. Cook lamb, uncovered, on heated oiled barbecue until cooked as desired. Add sesame seeds to marinade. Bring to boil on barbecue, simmer for 2 minutes or until thickened slightly. Serve lamb with black sesame seed dressing and Potato Almond Rosti.

Potato Almond Rosti Combine potato with remaining ingredients in medium bowl. Spread 1/4 cup measures of mixture on heated oiled barbecue plate; cook until browned both sides and crisp.

SERVES 4

BLACK BEAN LAMBURGERS

2 tablespoons salted black beans
500g minced lamb
1 tablespoon chopped fresh
  coriander leaves
1 cup (70g) stale breadcrumbs
1 egg, beaten lightly
3 medium (570g) tomatoes, chopped
1 small (100g) red onion, chopped
1 tablespoon peanut oil
4 crusty bread rolls
1 cup shredded lettuce leaves

Rinse beans under cold water 1 minute, drain; mash in large bowl. Add lamb, coriander, breadcrumbs and egg. Shape mixture into 4 patties. *[Best made ahead. Cover, refrigerate 3 hours or overnight.]*

Combine tomato, onion and oil in small bowl. Cook patties, uncovered, on heated oiled barbecue until browned both sides and cooked through. Split rolls; toast. Sandwich patties, tomato mixture and lettuce between roll halves.

MAKES 4

LAMB AND BURGHUL SAUSAGES

1/2 cup (80g) burghul
750g minced lamb
1/4 cup chopped fresh parsley
2 tablespoons chopped fresh
  mint leaves
1 tablespoon finely grated
  lemon rind
2 medium (380g) tomatoes,
  peeled, chopped
1 tablespoon ground cumin
1 tablespoon ground coriander
2 cloves garlic, crushed
1/2 cup (35g) stale breadcrumbs
1 egg, beaten lightly
2 large (400g) brown onions, sliced
1 cup (250ml) sour cream

Place burghul in small bowl, cover with cold water, stand 15 minutes; drain. Rinse burghul under cold water, drain; squeeze to remove excess moisture.

Combine burghul in large bowl with lamb, herbs, rind, tomato, cumin, coriander, garlic, breadcrumbs and egg. Using hands, shape 1/4 cup measures of mixture into sausages. *[Best made ahead. Cover, refrigerate 3 hours or overnight.]*

Cook sausages, in batches, on heated oiled barbecue, until browned all over and cooked through. Meanwhile, cook onion on heated barbecue until browned. Serve sausages with sour cream.

SERVES 4 TO 6

BUTTERMILK LAMB SAUSAGES WITH ONION JAM

1kg minced lamb
1/2 cup (125ml) buttermilk
2 tablespoons chopped fresh
  tarragon leaves
2 bird's-eye chillies, chopped
2 cloves garlic, crushed

ONION JAM
30g butter
3 large (600g) brown onions,
  sliced thinly
3/4 cup (180ml) brown malt vinegar
1/3 cup (75g) raw sugar

Combine lamb, buttermilk, tarragon, chilli and garlic in large bowl. *[Best made ahead. Cover, refrigerate at least 1 hour.]*

Using hands, shape 1/4 cup measures of mixture into sausages. Cook sausages on heated oiled barbecue until browned all over and cooked through. Serve with Onion Jam.

Onion Jam Melt butter in large pan; cook onion, vinegar and sugar over low heat, stirring occasionally, about 40 minutes or until mixture caramelises.

SERVES 4 TO 6

Left Lamb with black sesame seed dressing
Above, from left Lamb and burghul sausages; Buttermilk lamb sausages with onion jam; Black bean lamburgers

TANDOORI LAMB WITH INDIAN RICE SEASONING

You need about 1/3 cup uncooked rice for this recipe.

2 teaspoons vegetable oil
1 small (80g) white
   onion, chopped
1 clove garlic, crushed
2 teaspoons black mustard seeds
2 teaspoons cumin seeds
1 teaspoon ground coriander
1 cup cooked basmati rice
1/2 cup (35g) stale breadcrumbs
1 egg, beaten lightly
1 tablespoon lemon juice
1.25kg boned lamb shoulder
1/2 cup (125ml) yogurt
2 tablespoons tandoori paste

Heat oil in medium pan; cook onion and garlic, stirring, until onion is soft. Add seeds and coriander; cook, stirring, until seeds begin to pop. Combine spice mixture in medium bowl with rice, breadcrumbs, egg and juice. *[Can be made ahead to this stage. Cover, refrigerate overnight.]*

Fill cavity of lamb with rice seasoning; roll to enclose filling, tie with kitchen string. Brush lamb with combined yogurt and paste; place in disposable baking dish. Cook in covered barbecue, using indirect heat, following manufacturer's instructions, about 2 hours or until cooked as desired. Remove from heat, cover; stand 10 minutes before slicing and serving.

SERVES 4 TO 6

INDIAN SPICED LAMB WITH ALOO CHOP

1/4 cup (60ml) yogurt
1/4 cup (60ml) tandoori paste
1/4 cup (60ml) lime juice
3 cloves garlic, crushed
1 tablespoon grated fresh ginger
1 tablespoon garam masala
3 (900g) lamb eye of loin

ALOO CHOP

3 medium (600g) potatoes
30g butter
3/4 cup (180ml) sour cream
1/3 cup (50g) self-raising flour
1/2 teaspoon baking powder

Combine yogurt, paste, juice, garlic, ginger and garam masala in large bowl, add lamb; mix well. [Best made ahead. Cover, refrigerate overnight.]

Remove lamb from marinade; discard marinade. Cook lamb, uncovered, on heated oiled barbecue until cooked as desired. Serve lamb with Aloo Chop.

Aloo Chop Boil, steam or microwave potatoes until tender; drain. Mash potato, stir in remaining ingredients; mix well. Using hands, shape 1/4 cup measures of mixture into patties; cook, in batches, on heated oiled barbecue plate until browned both sides.

SERVES 4

CROWN ROAST WITH WILD RICE FILLING

1/2 cup (100g) white and wild rice blend
1/4 cup (60ml) olive oil
1 small (80g) white onion, chopped finely
2 cloves garlic, crushed
6 slices (90g) prosciutto, chopped

2 teaspoons chopped fresh rosemary
2 crown roasts of lamb (18 cutlets in 2 separate pieces)
2 tablespoons red wine vinegar
1 tablespoon Dijon mustard

Cook rice in large pan of boiling water, uncovered, about 12 minutes or until just tender; drain. Heat 1 tablespoon of the oil in medium pan; cook onion, garlic and prosciutto, stirring, until onion is soft. Stir in rice and rosemary. [Can be made ahead. Cover, refrigerate overnight.]

Tie lamb pieces together with kitchen string to resemble a crown. Carefully

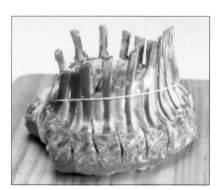

remove any skin or fat from bones at top. Place lamb roast in disposable baking dish or on large sheet of foil. Combine remaining oil, vinegar and mustard in jug; brush half of mixture over lamb. Place a small heatproof bowl in centre of roast to hold crown shape. Cover disposable baking dish with foil or gather foil around to cover roast completely. Cook in covered barbecue, using indirect heat, following manufacturer's instructions, 20 minutes.

Remove foil and heatproof bowl from centre of roast; spoon rice mixture into centre. Wrap any extra seasoning in foil and place alongside roast. Brush roast with remaining oil mixture. Cook, in covered barbecue, using indirect heat, about 30 minutes or until cooked as desired.

SERVES 4 TO 6

Left, from top Tandoori lamb with Indian rice seasoning; Indian spiced lamb with aloo chop
Below Crown roast with wild rice filling

ROSEMARY LAMB SKEWERS WITH SPICED YOGURT

Soak bamboo skewers in water for about 1 hour to prevent them scorching.

1kg lamb, cubed
1/4 cup (60ml) light olive oil
1 cup (250ml) dry red wine
2 tablespoons soy sauce
2 cloves garlic, crushed
2 tablespoons chopped fresh rosemary
1 teaspoon freshly ground black pepper
1 large (300g) red onion, chopped finely

SPICED YOGURT
200ml yogurt
1 tablespoon lemon juice
2 teaspoons ground cumin
1 teaspoon sugar

Place lamb in large shallow dish, add remaining ingredients, mix well. *[Best made ahead to this stage. Cover, refrigerate 3 hours or overnight.]*

Drain lamb; discard marinade. Thread lamb on 8 skewers; cook, uncovered, on heated oiled barbecue until browned all over and cooked as desired. Serve lamb with Spiced Yogurt.

Spiced Yogurt Combine all ingredients in small bowl. *[Best made ahead; cover, refrigerate 1 hour or overnight.]*

SERVES 4

LAMB WITH PISTACHIO HARISSA AND COUSCOUS

8 large (125g) red chillies, chopped
4 cloves garlic, chopped
1 tablespoon ground cumin
1 tablespoon ground coriander
2 teaspoons grated lemon rind
1 tablespoon lemon juice
1/4 cup (35g) shelled pistachios
1 tablespoon chopped fresh mint leaves
1 tablespoon chopped fresh coriander leaves
2 tablespoons olive oil
12 lamb cutlets

COUSCOUS
1 cup (200g) couscous
1 cup (250ml) boiling water
1 tablespoon olive oil
2 tablespoons sliced dried apricots
1 tablespoon finely chopped fresh flat-leaf parsley
2 tablespoons shelled chopped pistachios

Blend or process chilli, garlic, spices, rind, juice, nuts, leaves and oil until pureed. Place cutlets in large shallow dish; spread with half the harissa. *[Best made ahead to this stage. Cover, refrigerate 3 hours, or overnight.]*

Cook cutlets, uncovered, on heated oiled barbecue until browned both sides and cooked as desired. Serve cutlets with remaining harissa and Couscous.

Couscous Combine couscous and the water in medium heatproof bowl; cover, stand about 5 minutes or until water is absorbed. Using fork, fluff couscous gently; toss in remaining ingredients.

SERVES 4

Left, from top Rosemary lamb skewers with spiced yogurt; Lamb with pistachio harissa and couscous
Above Tomato and bocconcini lamb stacks

TOMATO AND BOCCONCINI LAMB STACKS

2 teaspoons olive oil
2 tablespoons balsamic vinegar
2 cloves garlic, crushed
24 French-trimmed lamb cutlets
3 large (270g) egg tomatoes, sliced
300g bocconcini cheese, sliced
2 tablespoons coarsely chopped fresh basil leaves

Combine oil, vinegar and garlic in small jug; brush over cutlets. Cook cutlets, uncovered, on heated oiled barbecue until brown on one side; remove, place on oven tray, cooked-side up. Layer tomato, bocconcini and basil on cooked side of 12 cutlets; top with remaining 12 cutlets, cooked-side down. Tie cutlets together with kitchen string; return to barbecue. Cook until browned both sides and cooked as desired.

SERVES 4 TO 6

Seafood

Life in the lucky country is even better for the vast majority of us who live close to the coast, so it's little wonder that seafood extravaganzas loom large at family get-togethers or special-occasion entertaining. Firm-fleshed fish are the best choice for the barbecue – select whole fish or thick steaks from the large deep-sea varieties for best results – and don't forget the wonderful appeal of barbecued calamari and prawns.

BALSAMIC-FLAVOURED OCTOPUS

1.5kg baby octopus
2 cloves garlic, crushed
1/4 cup (60ml) olive oil
1/4 cup (60ml) balsamic vinegar
1 tablespoon brown sugar
2 teaspoons chopped fresh thyme
150g curly endive
2 tablespoons olive oil, extra
2 tablespoons balsamic
vinegar, extra

Remove and discard heads and beaks from octopus; cut each octopus in half, combine in large bowl with garlic, oil, vinegar, sugar and thyme. *[Best made ahead to this stage. Cover, refrigerate 3 hours, overnight or freeze.]*

Drain octopus over small bowl; reserve marinade. Just before serving, cook octopus, in batches, on heated oiled barbecue, uncovered, until browned all over and just cooked through, brushing occasionally with reserved marinade. Serve with curly endive, drizzled with combined extra oil and extra vinegar.

SERVES 4 TO 6

SWORDFISH WITH OLIVE PASTE

200g black olives, seeded
1/4 cup (50g) drained capers
1/3 cup finely chopped fresh dill
1/3 cup finely chopped fresh
flat-leaf parsley
2 cloves garlic, crushed
2 tablespoons lemon juice
4 (800g) swordfish steaks

Blend or process olives, capers, dill, parsley, garlic and juice until almost a smooth paste. *[Best made ahead to this stage. Cover, refrigerate up to 3 days.]*

Cook steaks on heated oiled barbecue, uncovered, until browned both sides and just cooked through; spread tops with olive paste.

SERVES 4

From top Balsamic-flavoured octopus; Swordfish with olive paste

SEAFOOD BROCHETTES WITH LIME AND COCONUT

Soak bamboo skewers in water for about 1 hour to prevent them scorching. You need 24 skewers for this recipe.

500g piece tuna
500g piece salmon
500g piece swordfish
1/3 cup (90g) finely chopped palm sugar
400ml coconut cream
2 tablespoons grated kaffir lime rind
1/4 cup (60ml) kaffir lime juice
2 bird's-eye chillies, seeded, chopped finely

Remove any skin from fish; cut each fish into 4cm pieces. Place sugar and cream in small pan; stir over low heat, without boiling, until sugar dissolves, cool. Stir in rind, juice, chilli and fish. *[Best made ahead to this stage. Cover, refrigerate for 3 hours, overnight or freeze.]*

Drain fish over small pan; reserve marinade. Thread a mixture of fish pieces onto 12 pairs of skewers; grill on heated oiled barbecue, uncovered, until browned lightly and just cooked through. Place reserved marinade on barbecue; simmer, uncovered, 1 minute or until thickened slightly. Serve with brochettes.

MAKES 12

Plate, sushi plate and small cup from Dinosaur Designs

BLACKENED BLUE EYE WITH SWEET TOMATO RELISH

4 (800g) blue eye fillets
2 tablespoons olive oil
2 tablespoons grated fresh ginger
1 1/2 tablespoons ground turmeric
1 tablespoon garlic powder
1 tablespoon mustard powder
1 tablespoon sweet paprika
1 tablespoon dried basil leaves
1 tablespoon ground fennel
1/4 teaspoon cayenne pepper
1/4 teaspoon hot chilli powder
2 teaspoons salt

SWEET TOMATO RELISH
10 medium (750g) egg tomatoes, halved
2 cups (500ml) water
1/2 cup (125ml) dry white wine
1 tablespoon lime juice
1/2 cup (100g) firmly packed brown sugar
1 tablespoon grated lime rind
1 tablespoon ground turmeric
1 tablespoon yellow mustard seeds
2 bay leaves
2 stalks fresh lemon grass

Place fish in large shallow dish; pour over combined oil and ginger. *[Best made ahead to this stage. Cover, refrigerate for 3 hours or overnight.]*

Drain fish; discard marinade. Coat fish in combined remaining ingredients; cook on heated oiled barbecue, uncovered, until browned both sides and just cooked through. Serve with Sweet Tomato Relish.

Sweet Tomato Relish Combine all ingredients in medium saucepan. Simmer, uncovered, 30 minutes or until most of the liquid has evaporated. Cool, remove and discard leaves and lemon grass. *[Best made ahead. Cover, refrigerate up to 1 week.]*

SERVES 4

SEAFOOD PLATTER

500g baby octopus
500g medium uncooked prawns
12 (400g) scallops in shells
300g calamari rings
300g piece firm white boneless
fish, chopped
300g piece salmon
1/2 cup (125ml) olive oil
1/4 cup (60ml) balsamic vinegar
1/4 cup (35g) chopped drained
sun-dried tomatoes
2 tablespoons chopped fresh
oregano leaves
2 cloves garlic, crushed
1 tablespoon lime juice
3 (350g) uncooked Balmain
bugs, halved
12 (250g) small black mussels

Remove and discard heads and beaks from octopus; cut each octopus into quarters. Shell and devein prawns, leaving tails intact. Remove scallops from shells; reserve shells. Combine octopus, prawns, scallops, calamari and fish in large bowl with oil, vinegar, tomatoes, oregano, garlic and juice; mix well. [Best made ahead. Cover, refrigerate for 3 hours or overnight.]

Remove octopus, scallops, calamari, fish and salmon from marinade. Cook in batches, on heated oiled barbecue, uncovered, until browned all over and just cooked through. Slice salmon.

Remove prawns from marinade; discard marinade. Cook prawns and bugs on barbecue until browned both sides and just changed in colour. Cook mussels on barbecue until shells have opened. Return scallops to shells; serve seafood with Turkish bread and lemon or lime wedges, if desired.

SERVES 6

Far left Blackened blue eye with
sweet tomato relish
Left Seafood brochettes with lime
and coconut
Above Seafood platter

Above, from left Lemon and mustard calamari;
Tuna steaks with olive and fetta salsa;
Right Chilli lime snapper

LEMON AND MUSTARD CALAMARI

*You will need about 1¹/₃ cups (265g)
uncooked white rice for this recipe.*

1 tablespoon olive oil
**1 small (80g) white onion,
  chopped finely**
2 cloves garlic, crushed
4 green onions, chopped
4 cups cooked calrose rice
**¹/₂ cup (40g) coarsely grated
  parmesan cheese**
**1 tablespoon finely grated
  lemon rind**
1 egg, beaten lightly
1 tablespoon mild English mustard
6 medium (960g) calamari hoods

LEMON AND MUSTARD DRESSING
¹/₃ cup (80ml) olive oil
1 clove garlic, crushed
2 tablespoons lemon juice
2 teaspoons mild English mustard
¹/₂ teaspoon sugar

Heat oil in pan; cook white onion and
garlic, stirring, until onion is soft. Add
green onion; cook, stirring, until just
soft. Combine rice, onion mixture,
cheese, rind, egg and mustard in large
bowl. *[Can be made ahead to this stage.
Cover, refrigerate overnight.]*

  Spoon mixture into calamari hoods,
securing ends with toothpicks. Cook
calamari on heated oiled barbecue,
uncovered, until browned all over and
tender. Serve drizzled with Lemon and
Mustard Dressing.

Lemon and Mustard Dressing Combine
all ingredients in jar; shake well.

SERVES 4 TO 6

CHILLI LIME SNAPPER

- 2 (1kg) whole snapper
- 2 small bird's-eye chillies, seeded, sliced
- 2 tablespoons grated lime rind
- 2 tablespoons chopped fresh coriander leaves
- 2 fresh kaffir lime leaves, shredded
- 1 tablespoon sliced fresh lemon grass
- 1 tablespoon grated fresh ginger
- 2 teaspoons Sichuan pepper
- 3 green onions, sliced thinly
- 1 tablespoon fish sauce
- 1 tablespoon lime juice
- 1 tablespoon sesame oil

Cut fish 3 times on each side. Place each fish on a large piece of foil. Combine chilli, rind, coriander, lime leaves, lemon grass, ginger, pepper and onion in medium bowl; divide chilli mixture between fish. Combine sauce, juice and oil; pour over fish. Seal foil to enclose fish. *[Best made ahead to this stage. Cover, refrigerate 3 hours or overnight.]*

Place fish on heated oiled barbecue. Cook, covered, using indirect heat, following manufacturer's instructions, 10 minutes. Carefully turn fish over; cook about 10 minutes or until just cooked through.

SERVES 4

TUNA STEAKS WITH OLIVE AND FETTA SALSA

- 1 tablespoon olive oil
- 1 tablespoon lemon juice
- 1/4 teaspoon cracked black pepper
- 8 (1.6kg) tuna steaks

OLIVE AND FETTA SALSA
- 4 medium (760g) tomatoes, seeded, chopped
- 200g seeded black olives, sliced
- 300g fetta cheese, chopped
- 1/3 cup chopped fresh oregano leaves
- 2 tablespoons pine nuts, toasted

Combine oil, juice and pepper in small jug; brush over tuna. Cook tuna on heated oiled barbecue, uncovered, brushing occasionally with oil mixture, until browned both sides and just cooked through. Serve immediately with Olive and Fetta Salsa.

Olive and Fetta Salsa Combine all ingredients in small bowl.

SERVES 8

Star skewers from Made on Earth

LOBSTER TAILS WITH AVOCADO AND CAPSICUM

4 medium (1.5kg) uncooked
   lobster tails
40g butter, melted
2 cloves garlic, crushed

AVOCADO PUREE
2 medium (500g) avocados
1 tablespoon lime juice

RED CAPSICUM SAUCE
4 medium (800g) red capsicums
1 tablespoon olive oil
1 medium (150g) white
   onion, chopped
1 clove garlic, crushed
1/2 cup (125ml) chicken stock

Remove and discard skin from underneath lobster tails to expose flesh.

Cut each tail in half lengthways. Combine butter and garlic in small bowl; brush over lobster flesh. Cook lobster on heated oiled barbecue, uncovered, until browned both sides and changed in colour. Serve lobster with Avocado Puree and Red Capsicum Sauce.

Avocado Puree Blend or process avocados and juice until nearly smooth.

Red Capsicum Sauce Quarter capsicums; remove and discard seeds and membranes. Cook capsicum, skin-side-down, on heated oiled barbecue until skin blisters and blackens. Cover capsicum pieces in plastic or paper 5 minutes; peel away skin. Heat oil in small pan; cook onion and garlic, stirring, until onion is soft. Add capsicum and stock; bring to boil. Remove from heat; blend or process capsicum mixture until nearly smooth. *[Can be made a day ahead to this stage. Cover, refrigerate overnight.]*

SERVES 4

White oval plate from The Bay Tree

TUNA WITH CORIANDER PESTO

4 thick (800g) tuna steaks

CORIANDER PESTO
1/2 cup firmly packed fresh coriander leaves
1/4 cup (60ml) peanut oil
1 tablespoon unsalted roasted peanuts
1 small bird's-eye chilli, seeded, chopped
2 tablespoons lime juice
2 teaspoons wasabi paste

Reserving half the Coriander Pesto, brush tuna with remainder. Cook tuna on heated oiled barbecue, uncovered, until browned both sides and just cooked through. Serve tuna with reserved Coriander Pesto.

Coriander Pesto Blend or process coriander, oil, peanuts, chilli, juice and paste until just smooth. *[Best made ahead to this stage. Cover, refrigerate for 3 hours or overnight.]*

SERVES 4

SMOKED TROUT WITH POTATO AND APPLE WEDGES

You need 250g smoking chips for this recipe.

1 cup (250ml) apple juice
2 tablespoons grated lemon rind
4 (2kg) rainbow trout
1 medium (150g) white onion, sliced thinly
2 tablespoons finely chopped fresh thyme
1 tablespoon grated fresh ginger
1 tablespoon grated lemon rind, extra
1/3 cup (80ml) olive oil
4 medium (800g) potatoes
2 teaspoons sea salt
4 medium (600g) apples
1 large (300g) pink grapefruit, segmented
1 tablespoon sugar

Combine smoking chips, juice and rind in small bowl, stand 2 hours.

Cut 3 deep slits in each side of each fish. Combine onion, thyme, ginger, extra rind and half the oil; place a quarter of the onion mixture inside each cavity. Place fish in disposable baking dish. Place drained chips in smoke box; place on barbecue beside fish. Cook in covered barbecue, using indirect heat, following manufacturer's instructions, for about 30 minutes or until cooked through.

Meanwhile, peel potatoes, cut into wedges; place in disposable baking dish. Place potatoes on barbecue next to fish, sprinkle with salt, drizzle with remaining oil. Cook 20 minutes. Peel and core apples, cut into wedges. Place apple and grapefruit in dish with potato, sprinkle with sugar; cook 15 minutes or until potatoes and apples are tender.

SERVES 4

Left, from top Lobster tails with avocado and capsicum; Tuna with coriander pesto
Above Smoked trout with potato and apple wedges

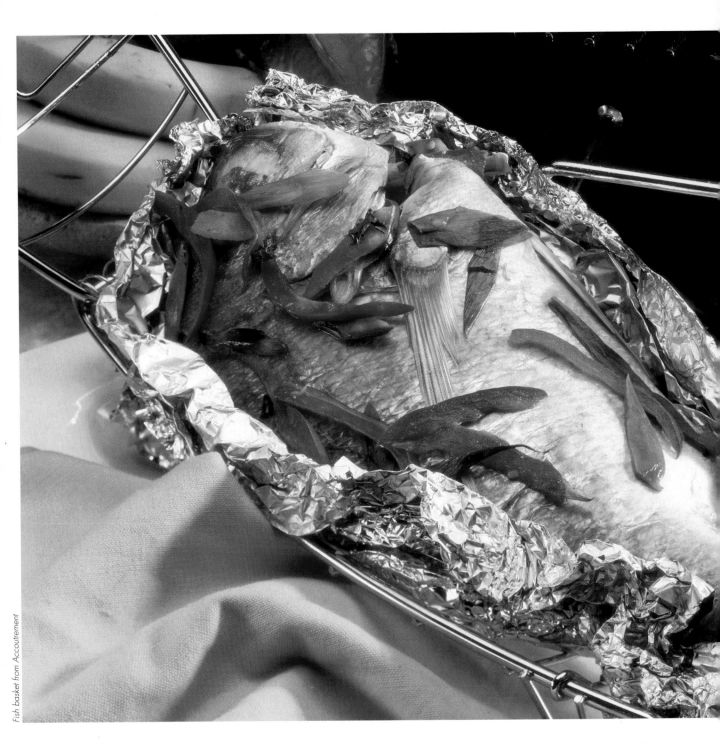

Fish basket from Accoutrement

SNAPPER FILLED WITH THAI-STYLE VEGETABLES

2 medium (400g) red capsicums, sliced thinly

6 green onions, sliced thinly

200g snow peas, sliced thinly

2 tablespoons thinly sliced fresh ginger

2 tablespoons sweet chilli sauce

2 teaspoons fish sauce

2 tablespoons lime juice

1/3 cup fresh basil leaves

1/2 cup fresh coriander leaves

1.5kg whole snapper

Combine capsicum, onion, snow peas, ginger, sauces, juice and herbs in medium bowl. Fill fish cavity with vegetable mixture. Wrap fish in oiled foil, place in fish grill, or on grill or plate. Cook in covered barbecue, using indirect heat, following manufacturer's instructions, about 45 minutes or until fish is just cooked through.

SERVES 4

TERIYAKI SNAPPER WITH SOBA

1/2 cup (125ml) soy sauce

1/4 cup (60ml) oyster sauce

2 tablespoons brown sugar

1/4 cup (60ml) mirin

4 thick (800g) snapper steaks

250g packet soba noodles

Combine sauces, sugar and mirin in large bowl; add fish. *[Best made ahead to this stage. Cover, refrigerate for 3 hours or overnight.]*

Drain fish over small pan; reserve marinade. Cook fish on heated oiled

COCO-LIME FISH WITH PAW PAW AND RASPBERRY SALSA

2 tablespoons finely chopped
  palm sugar
400ml coconut cream
2 tablespoons finely grated
  kaffir lime rind
2 bird's-eye chillies, chopped finely
4 thick (800g) snapper steaks

PAW PAW AND RASPBERRY SALSA
2 tablespoons raspberry vinegar
250g fresh raspberries
600g paw paw, chopped
1 tablespoon chopped fresh
  mint leaves

Combine sugar, cream, rind and chilli in small pan. Simmer, stirring occasionally, for 10 minutes; cool. Pour coconut mixture over fish in large bowl. *[Best made ahead to this stage. Cover, refrigerate for 3 hours or overnight.]*

Drain fish over small pan; reserve marinade. Cook fish, uncovered, on heated oiled barbecue until browned both sides and just cooked through. Meanwhile, place reserved marinade on barbecue, bring to boil; simmer, uncovered, until thickened slightly. Drizzle marinade over fish and serve with the Paw Paw and Raspberry Salsa.

Paw Paw and Raspberry Salsa Combine all ingredients in medium bowl; cover, refrigerate 30 minutes.

barbecue, uncovered, until browned both sides and just cooked through.

Meanwhile, place reserved marinade on barbecue, bring to boil, simmer, uncovered, 2 minutes. Cook noodles according to directions on packet; drain. Stir marinade through noodles. Serve fish on top of noodles.

SERVES 4

Right, from top Coco-lime fish with paw paw and raspberry salsa; Teriyaki snapper with soba
Above Snapper filled with Thai-style vegetables

GINGER TUNA WITH WASABI DRIZZLE

1/2 cup (125ml) olive oil
2 teaspoons grated fresh ginger
3 bird's-eye chillies, seeded, chopped finely
2 tablespoons chopped fresh lemon grass
4 thick (800g) tuna steaks

WASABI DRIZZLE
1 cup (250ml) white wine
2 tablespoons finely chopped palm sugar
1/3 cup (80ml) cider vinegar
1 tablespoon wasabi paste
300ml creme fraiche

Combine oil, ginger, chilli and lemon grass in large bowl; add tuna. [Best made ahead to this stage. Cover, refrigerate 3 hours or overnight.]

Drain tuna over small bowl; reserve marinade. Cook tuna on heated oiled barbecue, uncovered, brushing with reserved marinade, until browned both sides and just cooked through. Serve with Wasabi Drizzle.

Wasabi Drizzle Combine wine, sugar and vinegar in small pan; simmer, uncovered, until reduced by half, cool slightly. Stir in paste and creme fraiche. [Can be made ahead. Cover, refrigerate overnight.]

SERVES 4

ASIAN-STYLE SNAPPER IN BANANA LEAVES

4 large banana leaves
4 (1.5kg) bream or snapper
2 tablespoons grated fresh ginger
1/3 cup (about 1 stalk) thinly sliced fresh lemon grass
2 cloves garlic, crushed
1 tablespoon lime juice
2 tablespoons soy sauce
1/4 cup (60ml) sweet chilli sauce
1 teaspoon sesame oil
1 cup (80g) bean sprouts
225g baby bok choy, chopped
2 trimmed (150g) sticks celery, sliced
4 green onions, chopped

Cut each banana leaf into 35cm square. Using tongs, dip one leaf at a time into large pan of boiling water; remove immediately, rinse under cold water, dry thoroughly. Leaves should be soft and pliable.

Cut fish 3 times on each side. Place each fish on a square of leaf; top with ginger and lemon grass. Combine garlic, juice, sauces and oil; drizzle a little mixture over each fish. Fold leaves over fish; secure parcels with kitchen string. Place parcels on barbecue, seam-side-down. Cook in covered barbecue, using indirect heat, following manufacturer's instructions, about 25 minutes or until just cooked through.

Combine sprouts, bok choy, celery and onion with remaining sauce mixture. Cook on heated oiled barbecue, until just cooked and tender. Serve vegetable mixture with fish.

SERVES 4

Fork from The Bay Tree

Left Ginger tuna with wasabi drizzle
Opposite Asian-style snapper in banana leaves

Above Salmon with watercress and dill pesto
Right Garfish parcels with coriander salsa

SALMON WITH WATERCRESS AND DILL PESTO

1.5kg whole side salmon
1/2 cup (125g) mascarpone cheese

WATERCRESS AND DILL PESTO
**1/2 cup (50g) chopped
fresh watercress**
1/2 cup chopped fresh dill
1/2 cup (80g) pine nuts, toasted
**2/3 cup (50g) coarsely grated
parmesan cheese**
2 tablespoons grated lime rind
2 cloves garlic, crushed
1/3 cup (80ml) olive oil

Remove skin and bones from salmon. Place salmon on large sheet of foil; spread with Watercress and Dill Pesto, wrap in foil. Cook salmon, pesto-side-up, on heated oiled barbecue, uncovered, 15 minutes. Open foil; cook about 5 minutes or until salmon is just cooked through. Discard foil; cut salmon into 4 pieces, top with mascarpone cheese.

Watercress and Dill Pesto Blend or process watercress, dill, nuts, cheese, rind and garlic until just chopped. With motor operating, gradually pour in oil; process until thick. *[Can be made ahead. Cover, refrigerate up to 1 week.]*

SERVES 4

GARFISH PARCELS WITH CORIANDER SALSA

You will need about 3 corn cobs with the husks intact for this recipe. Cut base from corn cobs for easy removal of husks.

16 pieces corn husk
1 medium (200g) red capsicum
4 (400g) garfish
1 tablespoon finely grated lime rind

CORIANDER SALSA
2 medium (380g) tomatoes, seeded, chopped
1 small (100g) red onion, chopped finely
1 tablespoon lime juice
1 tablespoon olive oil
1 tablespoon coarsely chopped fresh coriander leaves

Cover husks with water in large bowl, cover, stand 3 hours or overnight; drain.

Quarter capsicum, remove seeds and membrane. Cook capsicum, skin-side-down, on heated oiled barbecue until skin blisters and blackens. Cover capsicum pieces in plastic or paper for 5 minutes, peel away skin, slice flesh. *[Can be made ahead. Cover, refrigerate overnight.]*

Using sharp scissors, cut backbone at tail end of each fish, flatten along backbone with rolling pin; gently peel out bone and discard.

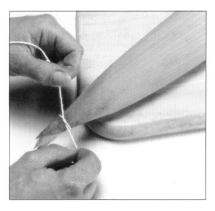

Wrap fish in husks with capsicum and rind; secure parcels with kitchen string. Cook fish parcels on heated oiled barbecue, uncovered, 5 minutes each side or until just cooked through. Serve with Coriander Salsa.

Coriander Salsa Combine all ingredients in small bowl.

SERVES 4

SARDINES IN CHERMOULLA WITH TOMATO SALSA

1/2 cup firmly packed fresh
 flat-leaf parsley
1/2 cup firmly packed fresh
 coriander leaves
4 cloves garlic, crushed
1 medium (170g) red
 onion, chopped
1 teaspoon grated lemon rind
1 teaspoon ground cumin
1 teaspoon sweet paprika
1 teaspoon grated fresh ginger
1/3 cup (80ml) peanut oil
24 (400g) fresh sardines, boned
4 medium (760g) tomatoes,
 seeded, chopped

Blend or process parsley, coriander, garlic, half the onion, rind, cumin, paprika, ginger and 1/4 cup of the oil until smooth. Reserve 2 tablespoons of the chermoulla. *[Best made ahead to this stage. Cover, refrigerate overnight.]*

Combine sardines with chermoulla in large bowl, cover; refrigerate 1 hour. Combine tomato, remaining onion, remaining oil and reserved chermoulla in small bowl. Cook sardines on heated oiled barbecue, uncovered, until sardines are browned both sides and just cooked through; serve with tomato salsa.

SERVES 6

TUNISIAN PRAWNS WITH CORIANDER POTATOES

1kg large uncooked prawns
1 teaspoon ground cumin
1 teaspoon ground coriander
1 teaspoon hot paprika
2 cloves garlic, crushed
2 eggs, beaten lightly
1 cup (150g) shelled pistachios,
 toasted, chopped finely

CORIANDER POTATOES
1 cup (25g) firmly packed fresh
 coriander leaves
1/3 cup (50g) pine nuts
1 clove garlic, crushed
2 tablespoons lime juice
1/4 cup (60ml) olive oil
4 large (1.2kg) potatoes

Shell and devein prawns, leaving tails intact. Place prawns in large shallow dish; add cumin, coriander, paprika and garlic, mix well. *[Best made ahead to this stage. Cover, refrigerate 3 hours or overnight.]*

Dip prawns in egg, coat in nuts; cook on heated oiled barbecue, uncovered, until browned both sides and changed in colour. Serve with Coriander Potatoes.

Coriander Potatoes Blend or process coriander, pine nuts, garlic and juice until just smooth. With motor operating, gradually add oil. *[Best made ahead to this stage. Cover, refrigerate for 3 hours or overnight.]*

Slice potatoes, brush with coriander mixture, place in disposable baking dish. Cook in covered barbecue, using indirect heat, following manufacturer's instructions, about 30 minutes or until potatoes are browned and tender.

SERVES 4

White bowls from The Bay Tree

SUGAR AND STAR-ANISE SMOKED SALMON

You need 300g heatbeads for this recipe.

1kg salmon fillet
1 cup (250ml) gin
2 tablespoons brown sugar
2 teaspoons mixed spice
2/3 cup (150g) white sugar
3/4 cup (40g) star anise
1 tablespoon dill seeds

Combine salmon, gin, brown sugar and mixed spice in large bowl. *[Best made ahead to this stage. Cover, refrigerate for 3 hours or overnight.]*

Place heatbeads in disposable baking dish; light heatbeads according to manufacturer's instructions. When flame has subsided and heatbeads have a coating of ash, sprinkle over white sugar, star anise and dill seeds. Drain salmon; discard marinade. Place salmon on wire rack over heatbeads; cover loosely with foil and cook in covered barbecue, using indirect heat, following manufacturer's instructions, about 20 minutes or until just cooked through.

SERVES 4 TO 6

Far left, from top Sardines in chermoulla with tomato salsa; Tunisian prawns with coriander potatoes
Above Sugar and star-anise smoked salmon
Above right Lemon grass and chilli-smoked swordfish

Glass plates and fork from Accoutrement; chair from The Edge Restaurant, Sydney

LEMON GRASS AND CHILLI-SMOKED SWORDFISH

1.5kg piece swordfish
1 tablespoon grated fresh ginger
4 fresh red bird's-eye chillies, chopped
1 cup (250ml) olive oil
3 stalks fresh lemon grass, pounded
1/2 cup (40g) lemon grass tea
1 litre (4 cups) boiling water
1 tablespoon dried chilli flakes

Cut swordfish into thick slices; combine with ginger, chilli, oil and a quarter of the lemon grass in large shallow dish. *[Best made ahead to this stage. Cover, refrigerate for 3 hours or overnight.]*

Combine tea, remaining lemon grass, water and chilli in large disposable baking dish; place on barbecue. Drain swordfish over a bowl; reserve marinade. Place swordfish on wire rack over large baking dish. Cook in covered barbecue, using indirect heat, following manufacturer's instructions, 35 minutes or until just cooked through. Brush occasionally with reserved marinade.

SERVES 4 TO 6

White bowl from The Bay Tree

Shell and devein prawns. Blend or process prawns, crab meat, chilli and ginger until well combined. Using hands, shape 1/4 cup measures of mixture into patties. *[Best made ahead to this stage. Cover, refrigerate 3 hours, overnight or freeze.]*

Just before serving, toss patties in flour, shaking away excess. Cook, uncovered, on heated, oiled barbecue until patties are browned both sides and cooked through. Serve with Sweet Chilli Cucumber Salsa.

Sweet Chilli Cucumber Salsa Combine all ingredients in small bowl.

MAKES 12

BUTTERFLIED HOT AND SOUR PRAWNS

1kg large uncooked prawns
1/4 cup (60ml) honey
1/4 cup (60ml) light soy sauce
1 tablespoon hoi sin sauce
2 cloves garlic, crushed
1 small bird's-eye chilli, seeded, chopped
2 teaspoons sesame seeds

Shell and devein prawns, leaving tails intact. Cut along prawn backs, lengthways, without separating halves. Combine honey, sauces, garlic and chilli in medium bowl with prawns. *[Best made ahead to this stage. Cover, refrigerate for 3 hours or overnight.]*

Cook flattened prawns on heated oiled barbecue, uncovered, until browned both sides and changed in colour. Serve sprinkled with toasted sesame seeds.

SERVES 4

SALMON WITH DILL AND CAPER MAYONNAISE

6 (1.5kg) salmon cutlets
2 tablespoons lemon pepper seasoning
2 tablespoons drained capers

DILL AND CAPER MAYONNAISE
2 egg yolks
1 tablespoon lemon juice
2 teaspoons Dijon mustard
1/2 cup (125ml) olive oil
1/2 cup (125ml) vegetable oil
1 tablespoon drained capers, chopped
1 tablespoon chopped fresh dill
1 tablespoon grated lemon rind

Sprinkle salmon all over with seasoning; cook, uncovered, on heated oiled barbecue until browned both sides and just cooked through. Cook capers on barbecue, uncovered, until well browned and crisp. Top salmon with capers and Dill and Caper Mayonnaise.

Dill and Caper Mayonnaise Blend or process egg yolks, juice and mustard until smooth. With motor operating, gradually pour in combined oils; process until thick. Stir in capers, dill and rind. *[Can be made ahead. Cover, refrigerate up to 3 days.]*

SERVES 6

CRAB AND PRAWN CAKES WITH SALSA

750g large uncooked prawns
500g shredded fresh crab meat
1 small bird's-eye chilli, seeded, chopped
1 teaspoon grated fresh ginger
plain flour

SWEET CHILLI CUCUMBER SALSA
4 small (520g) green cucumbers, seeded, chopped
1 medium (200g) red capsicum, seeded, chopped
1/4 cup (60ml) sweet chilli sauce
1 tablespoon fish sauce
1 tablespoon dry white wine
1 tablespoon brown sugar
2 tablespoons finely chopped fresh coriander leaves

Left Salmon with dill and caper mayonnaise
Right, from top Crab and prawn cakes with salsa; Butterflied hot and sour prawns

Pork

There's something special about pork sizzling on a barbecue. Crunchy crackling on a roast, simple pork sausages or a whole barbecued ham – whatever your favourite, there's a recipe here to please you. Serve your pork dish with sweet potatoes roasted over the fire, or an accompaniment of grilled fresh seasonal fruit... and remember that leftover pork loin makes a great sandwich the day after the barbecue.

PORK CHOPS WITH PEPPER AND BRANDY CREAM SAUCE

1 small (180g) pear, peeled, sliced
30g butter
1 medium (150g) onion, sliced
1 teaspoon brown sugar
1 tablespoon water
6 thick (1.7kg) pork chops

PEPPER AND BRANDY CREAM SAUCE
1/4 cup (60ml) brandy
2 tablespoons drained green peppercorns, crushed
1 cup (250ml) cream
1 tablespoon Worcestershire sauce

Cook pear on heated oiled barbecue until browned and tender. Melt butter in small pan on barbecue; cook onion, stirring, until browned lightly. Add pear, sugar and water; cook, stirring, until combined. Reserve a quarter of the pear mixture.

Cut small pocket in side of each chop; divide pear mixture among pockets, secure with toothpicks. Cook chops, uncovered, on heated oiled barbecue until browned both sides and cooked as desired. Serve with Pepper and Brandy Cream Sauce.

Pepper and Brandy Cream Sauce Place reserved pear mixture in medium pan; add brandy, simmer until reduced by half. Add peppercorns, cream and sauce; cook, stirring, until sauce thickens slightly.

SERVES 6

SAUSAGES WITH TOFFEED APPLE AND SWEET-SOUR LEEK

2 large (400g) red apples
1/3 cup (75g) firmly packed brown sugar
50g butter
2 large (1kg) leeks, sliced
2 cloves garlic, crushed
2 tablespoons red wine vinegar
12 thick (900g) pork sausages

Core apples; cut each into 12 wedges. Combine apple with half of the sugar in small bowl. Heat butter in medium pan on barbecue; cook leek and garlic, stirring, until soft. Add vinegar and remaining sugar; cook, stirring, about 10 minutes or until leek is soft and caramelised.

Cook sausages, in batches, uncovered, on heated oiled barbecue until browned all over and cooked through. Cook apples on heated oiled barbecue until browned both sides and just softened. Serve sweet-sour leek and toffeed apple with pork sausages.

SERVES 4 TO 6

From left Pork chops with pepper and brandy cream sauce; Sausages with toffeed apple and sweet-sour leek

GINGER PORK WITH MANGO AND RED ONION SALSA

2 tablespoons grated fresh ginger
1 tablespoon seeded mustard
1/3 cup (80ml) olive oil
4 (750g) pork butterfly steaks

MANGO AND RED ONION SALSA
2 medium (340g) red onions, sliced thinly
2 medium (860g) mangoes, sliced
2 tablespoons chopped fresh coriander leaves
1/4 cup (60ml) raspberry vinegar
2 teaspoons sugar

Combine ginger, mustard and oil in large bowl; add pork, mix well. *[Best made ahead to this stage. Cover, refrigerate at least 3 hours or overnight.]*

Drain pork; discard marinade. Cook, uncovered, on heated oiled barbecue until browned both sides and cooked as desired. Serve with Mango and Red Onion Salsa.

Mango and Red Onion Salsa Cook onion on heated oiled barbecue until browned and soft. Cook mango on heated oiled barbecue until browned all over. Combine onion and mango in medium bowl with remaining ingredients.

SERVES 4

MEDITERRANEAN PORK AND TAPENADE ROLL-UPS

2/3 cup (80g) seeded black olives
1/4 cup (60ml) olive oil
1 clove garlic, crushed
4 sun-dried tomatoes in oil, drained, chopped
1 tablespoon chopped fresh oregano leaves
1 tablespoon balsamic vinegar
1/4 cup (20g) coarsely grated parmesan cheese
8 (1.5kg) pork butterfly steaks
8 slices (120g) prosciutto

Blend or process olives, oil, garlic, tomato, oregano, vinegar and cheese until smooth. *[Can be made ahead to this stage. Cover, refrigerate overnight.]*

Place pork steaks between sheets of plastic wrap; pound with meat mallet until an even thickness. Divide olive paste into 8 equal portions; spread over surface of each steak, roll to enclose mixture. Wrap 1 slice of prosciutto around each roll; secure with toothpicks. Cook pork rolls, uncovered, on heated oiled barbecue, until browned all over and cooked as desired.

SERVES 8

ROAST LOIN OF PORK WITH CRACKLING AND APPLESAUCE

2kg boneless rolled loin of pork
2 tablespoons olive oil
2 tablespoons coarse cooking salt
6 medium (900g) apples
60g butter, softened
1/4 cup (50g) firmly packed
   brown sugar
2 teaspoons ground cinnamon

Place pork in disposable baking dish; drizzle with some of the oil, rub salt into skin. Cook in covered barbecue, using indirect heat, following manufacturer's instructions, 30 minutes. Brush with remaining oil; cook in covered barbecue about 45 minutes or until skin is browned and pork cooked as desired.

Meanwhile, peel, core and quarter apples. Divide among 4 sheets of foil; top with butter, sprinkle with sugar and cinnamon. Wrap foil to enclose apple mixture; place parcels on barbecue alongside pork for final 15 minutes of pork cooking time. Blend or process apples until thick. Serve applesauce with pork.

SERVES 6 TO 8

Plate from Sirocco Homewares; bowls from Orson & Blake

PORK STEAKS WITH CARAWAY CABBAGE

4 (800g) pork loin medallion steaks
2 rashers bacon, sliced thinly
1 medium (150g) onion,
   chopped finely
1 tablespoon caraway seeds
3 cups (240g) shredded cabbage
2 tablespoons brown sugar
1/4 cup (60ml) cider vinegar
40g butter
2 teaspoons finely chopped fresh
   sage leaves
2 tablespoons sour cream

Cook pork on heated oiled barbecue, un-covered, until browned both sides and cooked through. Meanwhile, cook bacon, onion and seeds in medium pan until onion is soft. Add cabbage, cook, stirring, 2 minutes. Stir in sugar, vinegar and butter, cook, stirring, about 3 minutes or until cabbage is soft. Just before serving, stir in sage. Serve pork topped with cabbage and sour cream.

SERVES 4

Far left, from top Mediterranean pork and tapenade roll-ups; Ginger pork with mango and red onion salsa
Left Roast loin of pork with crackling and applesauce
Above Pork steaks with caraway cabbage

STICKY RIBS WITH BOSTON BAKED BEANS

1/2 cup (125ml) barbecue sauce
1/4 cup (60ml) tomato sauce
2 tablespoons Worcestershire sauce
2 tablespoons mild chilli sauce
2 tablespoons honey
1kg pork spareribs
2 cups (500g) great northern beans
1 medium (150g) brown
    onion, chopped
1 bay leaf
1/2 cup (100g) firmly packed
    brown sugar
1/4 cup (60ml) American mustard
1/2 cup (125ml) molasses
2 cups (500ml) water
1 teaspoon salt
200g chopped bacon pieces

Combine sauces and honey in large bowl, add ribs, mix well; cover, refrigerate overnight. Place beans in large bowl, cover with cold water; stand overnight.

Drain and rinse beans, place in large pan with onion and bay leaf. Cover bean mixture with cold water, bring to boil, simmer, uncovered, about 50 minutes or until beans are tender. Drain beans, discard bay leaf.

Place beans in disposable baking dish, stir in sugar, mustard, molasses, water and salt; sprinkle with bacon. Drain ribs over small bowl; reserve marinade. Place ribs in disposable baking dish. Cook ribs and beans in covered barbecue, using indirect heat, following manufacturer's instructions, about 45 minutes or until ribs are tender and beans are slightly syrupy. During cooking, brush ribs occasionally with reserved marinade.

SERVES 4

CHILLI PLUM RIBS AND SPICY POTATO WEDGES

1/2 cup (125ml) plum sauce
2 tablespoons hot chilli sauce
1 tablespoon tomato sauce
1 tablespoon brown sugar
1kg pork ribs

SPICY POTATO WEDGES
1 tablespoon olive oil
1 teaspoon cajun seasoning
2 teaspoons garlic salt
6 medium (1.2kg) potatoes

Combine sauces and sugar in small bowl; brush ribs with marinade. [Best made ahead to this stage. Cover, refrigerate for 3 hours or overnight.]

Place ribs in disposable baking dish; reserve any marinade in bowl. Cook ribs and Spicy Potato Wedges in covered barbecue, using indirect heat, following manufacturer's instructions, about 45 minutes or until cooked through. During cooking, brush ribs occasionally with reserved marinade. Serve ribs with Spicy Potato Wedges.

Spicy Potato Wedges Combine oil, seasoning and garlic salt in large bowl. Cut each potato into 6 wedges; toss through oil mixture. Stand wedges skin-side-down in oiled disposable baking dish.

SERVES 4

TEX-MEX RIBS WITH CORN MUFFINS

1/2 cup (125ml) barbecue sauce
1 teaspoon chilli powder
35g taco seasoning
1kg pork spareribs

CORN MUFFINS
1 tablespoon olive oil
1 small (150g) red capsicum,
    chopped
1 clove garlic, crushed
1/2 cup (75g) self-raising flour
1 cup (170g) polenta
1/2 teaspoon bicarbonate of soda
130g can corn kernels, drained
1 tablespoon chopped fresh
    coriander leaves
1/2 cup (125ml) buttermilk
60g butter, melted
1 egg, beaten lightly

Combine sauce, chilli powder and seasoning in large bowl; add ribs, mix well. [Best made ahead to this stage. Cover, refrigerate for 3 hours or overnight.]

Place ribs in disposable baking dish. Cook in covered barbecue, using indirect heat, following manufacturer's instructions, 15 minutes. Place Corn Muffins next to ribs, continue to cook, covered, about 30 minutes or until ribs are tender and muffins cooked through. During cooking, brush ribs occasionally with pan juices. Serve with Corn Muffins.

Corn Muffins Heat oil in medium pan, add capsicum and garlic; cook, stirring, until capsicum is tender. Combine flour, polenta and soda in large bowl. Stir in capsicum mixture, corn and coriander, then stir in buttermilk, butter and egg. Divide mixture evenly among 4 greased muffin pans (1 cup/250ml capacity).

SERVES 4

Ribs, clockwise from centre Sticky ribs with Boston baked beans; Chilli plum ribs and spicy potato wedges; Tex-Mex ribs with corn muffins

ORANGE GLAZED HAM

6kg cooked leg of ham
2 small (360g) oranges,
   halved, sliced
whole cloves

ORANGE GLAZE
1/2 cup (125ml) orange marmalade
3/4 cup (180ml) orange juice
1/4 cup (50g) firmly packed
   brown sugar
2 teaspoons Dijon mustard
2 tablespoons Cointreau or
   Grand Marnier

Make a decorative cut through ham rind about 10cm from the shank end of leg. Make a shallow cut down centre of ham from one end to the other. Place ham on roasting rack or basket, or in disposable baking dish. Cook in covered barbecue, using indirect heat, following manufacturer's instructions, about 45 minutes or until skin begins to split. Remove from barbecue; cool 15 minutes. Peel skin away from ham carefully, leaving shank end intact; discard skin. Do not cut through surface of top fat or fat will spread during cooking. Secure orange slices with cloves in decorative pattern on ham. Wrap shank in foil; brush ham with Orange Glaze. Cook, covered, brushing occasionally with glaze, about 1 hour or until orange slices are lightly caramelised and ham is heated through.

Orange Glaze Mix all ingredients in small pan; stir over low heat until marmalade melts. *[Can be made ahead.]*

SERVES 12

THREE-PEPPER PORK

1 tablespoon black peppercorns
2 tablespoons green peppercorns
2 tablespoons ground lemon pepper
1/3 cup loosely packed fresh
   sage leaves
1.5kg boneless pork loin
3 cups (750ml) water

Process peppers and sage in spice grinder or blender until finely ground. Place pork, skin-side-down, on board; press pepper mixture over surface of meat. Roll from long side; tie with kitchen string at 2cm intervals. *[Can be made ahead to this stage. Cover, refrigerate for 3 hours or overnight, or freeze.]*

Score pork skin; place in disposable baking dish with the water. Cook in covered barbecue, using indirect heat, following manufacturer's instructions, about 1 1/2 hours or until browned all over and cooked as desired.

SERVES 4 TO 6

PORK WITH ARTICHOKE AND SPINACH LOG

1/3 cup (80ml) olive oil
1 clove garlic, crushed
2 tablespoons finely chopped
fresh thyme
4 (800g) pork tenderloins
3 large (900g) potatoes,
peeled, chopped
40g butter
1 medium (150g) brown onion,
chopped finely
1 clove garlic, crushed, extra
1kg spinach, trimmed
400g can artichoke hearts,
drained, chopped
2 cups (500ml) water
2 cups (500ml) dry red wine

Combine oil, garlic and thyme in large shallow dish; add pork, mix well. *[Best made ahead to this stage. Cover, refrigerate 3 hours or overnight.]*

Boil, steam or microwave potatoes until tender; drain, mash. Meanwhile, melt butter in medium pan; cook onion and extra garlic, stirring, until onion is soft. Place spinach in large heatproof bowl, cover with boiling water; drain, pat dry on absorbent paper. Combine potato and onion mixture in large bowl with artichoke hearts.

Place a piece of plastic wrap on bench; arrange spinach leaves in a 20cm x 30cm rectangle on plastic wrap. Spoon artichoke mixture along centre of spinach; fold one long side of spinach back over artichoke mixture to enclose it. Using plastic wrap as a guide, carefully roll to form log; twist ends tightly to hold shape. *[Best made ahead to this stage. Cover, refrigerate 3 hours or overnight.]*

Pour the water and wine into disposable baking dish. Drain pork; discard marinade. Place pork on wire rack over baking dish; cook in covered barbecue, using indirect heat, following manufacturer's instructions, about 30 minutes.

Meanwhile, remove plastic from artichoke and spinach log; wrap in foil, place on barbecue alongside pork for final 15 minutes of pork cooking time. Remove from barbecue when pork is cooked as desired and log heated through. Slice pork; cut log diagonally into 3cm slices.

SERVES 4

Left Orange glazed ham
Right, from top Three-pepper pork;
Pork with artichoke and spinach log

Vegetables

Don't overcook your vegetables – they should retain a bit of crunch in the mouth while acquiring that subtle charred smokiness from the barbecue that makes this such a change from your everyday method of cooking them. These recipes make delicious meals in themselves, singly for lunch, or combined for a family meal. They also make great accompaniments, adding interest to meat dishes.

GARLIC CHILLI POTATO KEBABS

Soak bamboo skewers in water about 1 hour to prevent them scorching.

24 tiny (960g) new potatoes, unpeeled
12 baby (300g) onions
14 bird's-eye chillies
2 cloves garlic, crushed
2 tablespoons olive oil

Boil, steam or microwave potatoes and onions separately until just tender; drain. *[Can be made ahead to this stage. Cover, refrigerate overnight.]*
   Thread potatoes, onions and 12 of the chillies onto 4 skewers. Finely chop remaining chillies. Combine chilli in small bowl with garlic and oil. Cook kebabs on heated oiled barbecue, brushing with chilli mixture occasionally, until kebabs are browned all over and tender.

SERVES 4

CARROT AND DILL ROSTI

1/2 cup (125ml) light sour cream
1 teaspoon ground cumin
1 tablespoon chopped fresh dill
5 medium (600g) carrots, grated
2 eggs, beaten lightly
1/3 cup (50g) plain flour

Combine sour cream, cumin and dill in small bowl. *[Can be made a day ahead. Cover, refrigerate overnight.]*
   Combine carrot, eggs and flour in large bowl. Cook 1/4 cup measures of carrot mixture in batches on heated oiled barbecue plate, until rostis are browned both sides. Serve rostis with the sour cream mixture.

MAKES ABOUT 8

Right Garlic chilli potato kebabs; Carrot and dill rosti

BAKED RICOTTA WITH CHAR-GRILLED VEGETABLES

4 cups (800g) ricotta cheese
3 eggs, beaten lightly
2 tablespoons olive oil
1/2 teaspoon dried chilli flakes

CHAR-GRILLED VEGETABLES
1 large (350g) red
  capsicum, quartered
1 large (350g) green
  capsicum, quartered
1 large (500g) eggplant, sliced
3 large (450g) zucchini, sliced
4 small (240g) egg
  tomatoes, quartered
2 medium (280g) lemons, quartered
3 small (300g) red
  onions, quartered
1/3 cup (80ml) olive oil
1 tablespoon cracked black pepper

Combine ricotta with eggs in medium bowl; pour into greased 24cm springform tin. Drizzle ricotta with oil, sprinkle with chilli. Cover lightly with foil, cook in covered barbecue, using indirect heat, following manufacturer's instructions, for 15 minutes. Remove foil, cook about for 10 minutes or until browned. Drain excess liquid from tin; cut ricotta into wedges. Serve with Char-grilled Vegetables.

Char-grilled Vegetables Combine all ingredients in large bowl. Cook vegetables on heated oiled barbecue, uncovered, until browned and tender.

SERVES 6 TO 8

CORN WITH SAGE AND BACON

4 (1.6kg) corn cobs
20 cups (5 litres) water
1/4 cup (60ml) milk
2 tablespoons chopped fresh
  sage leaves
2 bacon rashers, sliced thinly

Peel husks back from corn, leaving them attached at base; remove silk, fold husks back over corn. Soak corn in combined water and milk. *[Best made ahead. Cover, refrigerate for 3 hours or overnight.]*

Gently peel husk back from corn, press combined sage and bacon onto corn; tie husks with kitchen string to enclose filling. Place corn on grill rack. Cook in covered barbecue, using indirect heat, following manufacturer's instructions, about 40 minutes or until tender.

SERVES 4

Left Baked ricotta with char-grilled vegetables
Right, from top Corn with sage and bacon;
Potatoes with raclette cheese and garlic

POTATOES WITH RACLETTE CHEESE AND GARLIC

12 medium (1.5kg) kipfler potatoes
1 bulb garlic
40g butter
**2 cups (250g) grated
    raclette cheese**

Wrap potatoes and whole garlic individually in foil. Place in disposable baking dish. Cook in covered barbecue, using indirect heat, following manufacturer's instructions, 30 minutes or until garlic is tender; remove garlic. Cook potatoes another 20 minutes or until tender. Cut garlic in half; squeeze out pulp into small bowl; stir in butter.

Partially unwrap potatoes; cut lengthways down centre, not cutting all the way through potato or foil. Open out potatoes, cup foil around them. Divide butter mixture among potatoes; top with cheese. Place in baking dish. Cook in covered barbecue, using indirect heat, following manufacturer's instructions, for 20 minutes or until cheese melts and bubbles.

SERVES 6

MUSTARD HONEY GLAZED VEGETABLES

500g bunch baby carrots
600g bunch baby beetroot
500g bunch baby turnips
600g bunch spring onions
40g butter
¹/₄ cup (60ml) honey

2 tablespoons seeded mustard
1 tablespoon lemon juice

Trim peeled carrots, beetroot, turnips and onions, leaving 3cm of stems remaining. Combine remaining ingredients in small pan, stir over low heat until butter has melted. Combine vegetables in disposable baking dish with honey mixture. Cook in covered barbecue, using indirect heat, following manufacturer's instructions, for 40 minutes or until browned and tender.

SERVES 4 TO 6

Above Mustard honey glazed vegetables
Right, from top Mixed vegetables; Tomatoes with fetta, olives and polenta

MIXED VEGETABLES

2 medium (240g) yellow zucchini
2 medium (240g) green zucchini
1 large (350g) red capsicum
1 large (350g) yellow capsicum
4 medium (240g) baby eggplant
4 (100g) spring onions
200g haloumi cheese, sliced thinly
1 cup (250ml) olive oil
1 tablespoon caraway seeds, toasted
1 tablespoon grated lemon rind
1 clove garlic, crushed
2 teaspoons ground cumin
1 tablespoon finely chopped fresh
  lemon thyme
2 tablespoons finely
  chopped capers

Slice all vegetables thickly lengthways. Cook vegetables and cheese on heated oiled barbecue, uncovered, until browned both sides and tender. Transfer vegetables to large serving platter; drizzle with combined oil, seeds, rind, garlic, cumin, thyme and capers. Serve vegetables topped with cheese.

SERVES 6

TOMATOES WITH FETTA, OLIVES AND POLENTA

80g fetta cheese, crumbled
1 clove garlic, crushed
1 tablespoon olive oil
1 tablespoon finely chopped fresh
  lemon thyme
4 large (1kg) tomatoes
2/3 cup (80g) seeded black olives,
  sliced finely
1 tablespoon polenta

Combine cheese, garlic, oil and thyme in small bowl. *[Can be made ahead to this stage. Cover, refrigerate at least 3 hours or overnight.]*
  Cut tomatoes in half horizontally; cut small slice from base so tomato halves sit flat. Cook, cut-side-down, on heated oiled barbecue until browned lightly. Transfer tomatoes, cut-side-up, to disposable baking dish. Top tomatoes with olives, fetta mixture and polenta. Cook in covered barbecue, using indirect heat, following manufacturer's instructions, for 20 minutes or until browned.

SERVES 8

Dressed for success

A dressing adds its individual flavour to both salads and vegetables cooked on a barbecue. Here are a few classics, plus some of our favourites. At right, a chart that will make barbecuing vegetables a breeze.

HONEY DIJON DRESSING

1/4 cup (60ml) honey
2 tablespoons Dijon mustard
1/2 cup (125ml) white wine vinegar
1 tablespoon lemon juice
1 cup (250ml) peanut oil

Combine honey, mustard, vinegar and juice in small bowl. Gradually whisk in oil; continue to whisk until dressing is slightly thickened and smooth.

MAKES ABOUT 2 CUPS (500ml)

THOUSAND ISLAND DRESSING

1 cup (250ml) mayonnaise
1/4 cup (60ml) tomato paste
1/4 cup (60ml) tomato sauce
2 teaspoons Worcestershire sauce
1/2 teaspoon Tabasco sauce

Combine all ingredients in small bowl; whisk until smooth. Cover, refrigerate until required.

MAKES ABOUT 1 1/2 CUPS (375ml)

ROBBY'S DRESSING

2/3 cup (160ml) extra virgin
   olive oil
2 shallots, chopped
2 tablespoons balsamic vinegar
2 tablespoons white vinegar
2 tablespoons lemon juice
2 teaspoons sugar
2 cloves garlic, crushed
2 teaspoons Dijon mustard

Blend or process all ingredients until thickened slightly and smooth.

MAKES ABOUT 1 1/2 CUPS (375ml)

FRENCH DRESSING

1/2 cup (125ml) olive oil
1 tablespoon white wine vinegar
2 teaspoons Dijon mustard
1/2 teaspoon sugar

Combine all ingredients in jar; shake well.

MAKES ABOUT 2/3 CUP (160ml)

ITALIAN DRESSING

1/2 cup (125ml) white vinegar
1 tablespoon lemon juice
1 teaspoon sugar
1/2 cup (125ml) light olive oil
1 clove garlic, crushed
1/2 small (40g) white onion,
   chopped finely
1/2 small (75g) red capsicum,
   chopped finely
1/4 cup chopped fresh flat-leaf
   parsley leaves

Combine all ingredients in jar; shake well.

MAKES ABOUT 1 1/2 CUPS (375ml)

RUSSIAN DRESSING

1 cup (250ml) mayonnaise
1/4 cup (60ml) lemon juice
1/4 cup finely chopped gherkins
1 teaspoon sweet paprika
2 cloves garlic, crushed
1 tablespoon chopped fresh dill

Combine all ingredients in jar; shake well.

MAKES ABOUT 1 1/2 CUPS (375ml)

CAESAR SALAD DRESSING

6 drained anchovy fillets
1 clove garlic, crushed
2 teaspoons Dijon mustard
2 teaspoons white vinegar
1 teaspoon sugar
1 egg yolk
1/2 cup (125ml) vegetable oil
1/2 cup (125ml) buttermilk

Blend or process anchovies, garlic, mustard, vinegar, sugar and egg yolk until combined. With motor operating, gradually add oil and buttermilk; process until thickened and smooth.

MAKES ABOUT 1 1/2 CUPS (375ml)

VEGETABLE COOKING CHART

	Direct Heat	*Indirect Heat*
Artichokes	Boil, uncovered, 30 minutes, remove outer leaves, cut in half, remove hairy choke; barbecue until tender.	Boil, uncovered, 15 minutes, remove outer leaves and hairy choke, wrap in foil; barbecue until tender.
Asparagus	Brush or spray with oil; barbecue until tender.	
Baby bok choy	Cut in half lengthways, brush or spray with oil; barbecue until tender.	Wrap whole baby bok choy in greased foil; barbecue until tender.
Beans (green, butter, snake)	Wrap in foil with a little butter; barbecue until tender. Or, cook directly on barbecue plate until tender.	
Beetroot		Wrap whole unpeeled beetroot in foil; barbecue until tender then peel. Or, combine peeled, chopped beetroot with a little oil in a disposable baking dish; barbecue until tender.
Brussels sprouts	Cut in half, brush or spray with oil; barbecue until tender.	Wrap about 6 in foil with a little butter; barbecue until tender.
Capsicums	Quarter capsicums, remove seeds and membranes; barbecue, skin-side-down, until tender.	Place whole or filled capsicums in baking dish; barbecue until tender. Or, wrap in foil; barbecue until tender.
Carrots	Cut carrots in half lengthways; boil, steam or microwave until almost tender; barbecue until tender.	Chop or slice carrots, combine with a little oil in a baking dish; barbecue until tender. Or, wrap whole baby carrots in foil; cook on warming rack until tender.
Corn	Soak unpeeled corn in cold water overnight; barbecue in husks until tender. Or, barbecue thick slices of corn until tender.	Wrap in foil; barbecue until tender.
Eggplants	Cut into 1cm slices, brush or spray with oil; barbecue until tender.	Prick whole eggplants all over with a skewer, barbecue in lightly oiled baking dish until tender; peel, chop flesh.
Fennel	Cut into slices; cook with a little butter on barbecue plate until tender.	Cut in half or slice, combine with a little oil in a baking dish; barbecue until tender.
Leeks	Cut in half lengthways; barbecue until tender. Or, slice and cook on barbecue plate until tender.	Cut in half lengthways or roughly chop, combine with a little oil in a baking dish; barbecue until tender.
Mushrooms	Brush or spray with oil; barbecue until tender.	Can be left whole or cut in half, combine mushrooms with a little oil in a baking dish; barbecue until tender.
Onions	Slice or chop; cook with a little oil on barbecue plate. Or, cut unpeeled onions in half; barbecue on grill plate until tender.	Peel and wrap whole onions in foil; barbecue until tender. Or, can be chopped or sliced and combined with a little oil in a baking dish; barbecue until tender.
Parsnips, turnips		Chop or slice, combine with a little oil in a baking dish; barbecue until tender.
Potato, kumara	Cut into thin slices, brush or spray with oil; barbecue until tender.	Barbecue whole wrapped in foil until tender. Or, can be chopped or sliced and combined with a little oil in a baking dish; barbecue until tender.
Pumpkin	Cut unpeeled pumpkin into thin slices, brush or spray with oil; barbecue until tender.	Chop or slice pumpkin, combine with a little oil in a baking dish; barbecue until tender. Golden nugget can be wrapped in foil; barbecue until tender.
Swedes	Cut into thin slices, brush or spray with oil; barbecue until tender.	Wrap whole swede in foil; barbecue until tender. Or, can be chopped or sliced and combined with a little oil in a baking dish; barbecue until tender.
Tomatoes	Cut in half, brush or spray with oil; barbecue until tender.	Cut tomatoes in half, combine with a little oil in a baking dish; barbecue until tender.
Zucchini	Cut unpeeled zucchini in halves lengthways, brush or spray with oil; barbecue until tender.	Chop or slice, combine with a little oil in a baking dish; barbecue until tender. Or, wrap whole zucchini in foil; cook on warming rack until tender.

Breads and Desserts

Sweets and breads aren't the first things that come to mind when we think of barbecuing. But it's surprising how well they take to this method of cooking. Fruits, in particular, develop a deeper, richer flavour when grilled, while "baking" in a covered barbecue is similar to the conditions you find with old-fashioned, wood-fired ovens. This creates crusty breads and lends them a lovely, smoky character.

CHAR-GRILLED FRUITS

You will need about 3 passionfruit for this recipe.

1/2 medium (600g) pineapple
2 (200g) starfruit
2 small (260g) bananas
2 medium (860g) mangoes
2/3 cup (160ml) Malibu
1/4 cup (60ml) passionfruit pulp
1 tablespoon brown sugar
600ml thickened cream, whipped
2 tablespoons flaked
   coconut, toasted

Remove and discard top and base from pineapple; cut pineapple into 1cm-thick slices, cut each slice in half. Cut starfruit into 1cm-thick slices. Slice bananas in half lengthways. Cut mangoes down each side of stones; cut a criss-cross pattern into flesh.

Combine Malibu, 2 tablespoons of the passionfruit pulp and sugar in medium pan. Stir over low heat, without boiling, until sugar dissolves. Bring to boil; simmer, uncovered, 5 minutes. Reserve 2 tablespoons of the passionfruit syrup. Combine fruit with remaining passionfruit syrup in large bowl. Cook fruit, in batches, on heated oiled barbecue, brushing occasionally with syrup, until browned both sides and tender. Combine reserved passionfruit syrup with remaining passionfruit pulp in small jug. Drizzle warm fruit with passionfruit syrup. Serve fruit with cream sprinkled with coconut.

SERVES 6 TO 8

Jug from Shack; green tumbler from Empire Homewares; blue plate and pearl spoon from The Bay Tree Kitchen Shop; barbecue from Kangaroo Tent-City & BBQ's

DAMPER

3 cups (450g) self-raising flour
1 teaspoon salt
90g butter
1/2 cup (125ml) milk
1/2 cup (125ml) water,
approximately

Combine flour and salt in bowl; rub in butter. Pour in milk and enough water to mix to a soft, sticky dough. Turn dough onto floured surface; knead lightly. Knead dough into a round shape, place in disposable baking dish. Press dough into a 15cm round. Using a sharp knife, cut a cross in top of dough about 1cm deep. Brush top of dough with a little extra milk, sift a little extra flour over top. Cook in covered barbecue, using indirect heat, following manufacturer's instructions, about 35 minutes or until damper sounds hollow when tapped.

SERVES 6 TO 8

PUMPKIN AND WALNUT DAMPER

You will need to cook about 600g pumpkin for this recipe.

3 cups (450g) self-raising flour
50g butter
1 cup (120g) chopped walnuts
11/2 cups cooked mashed pumpkin
1/2 cup (125ml) buttermilk,
approximately

Grease 20cm round sandwich cake pan. Place flour in medium bowl; rub in butter, stir in nuts, pumpkin and enough buttermilk to mix to a soft, sticky dough. Turn dough onto floured surface, knead until smooth. Place into prepared pan. Cook in covered barbecue, using indirect heat, following manufacturer's instructions, about 30 minutes or until damper sounds hollow when tapped.

SERVES 4 TO 6

BOSTON BROWN BREAD

1 cup (170g) polenta
1 cup (125g) rye flour
1 cup (160g) wholemeal plain flour
2 teaspoons bicarbonate of soda
1 teaspoon salt
2 cups (500ml) buttermilk
3/4 cup (180ml) molasses
1 cup (170g) raisins

Combine polenta, flours, soda and salt in medium bowl; stir in buttermilk, molasses and raisins. Spoon mixture into greased 14cm x 21cm loaf pan. Cover top of pan with greased baking paper; cover tightly with a sheet of foil. Stand pan in disposable baking dish, pour in enough boiling water to come halfway up sides of pan; cover baking dish with foil. Cook in covered barbecue, using indirect heat, following manufacturer's instructions, about 2 hours or until bread is cooked when tested. Stand bread in pan for 5 minutes before turning onto wire rack to cool.

SERVES 4 TO 6

MIXED SEED BEER BREAD

31/4 cups (485g) self-raising flour
2 teaspoons salt
2 teaspoons sugar
1/2 cup (80g) sunflower
    seed kernels
2 tablespoons poppyseeds
1/2 cup (75g) sesame seeds
1/2 cup (90g) linseeds
375ml beer

Combine flour, salt and sugar in medium bowl, stir in seeds; pour in beer all at once. Using spoon, mix to a soft, sticky dough. Knead on a floured surface until smooth. Shape into a 12cm x 40cm rectangle, place in oiled disposable baking dish or on oiled foil. Using a sharp knife, make 3 shallow cuts across top of dough. Cook in covered barbecue, using indirect heat, following manufacturer's instructions about 1 hour or until bread is browned and sounds hollow when tapped.

SERVES 6 TO 8

Above, from left Mixed seed beer bread;
Boston brown bread
Right, from top Pumpkin and walnut damper;
Damper; Peppered spinach and fetta damper

PEPPERED SPINACH AND FETTA DAMPER

3¹/₂ cups (525g) self-raising flour
1 teaspoon salt
2 teaspoons cracked black pepper
1 tablespoon sugar
40g butter
1 cup (200g) fetta
   cheese, crumbled
3 cups (210g) baby spinach
   leaves, chopped
¹/₂ cup (125g) buttermilk
1 cup (250ml) water, approximately

Combine flour, salt, pepper and sugar in large bowl; rub in butter. Stir in cheese, spinach, buttermilk and enough water to make a soft, sticky dough. Turn dough onto floured surface, knead until just smooth. Divide dough in half, place in greased disposable baking dish, press each half into a 10cm round. Cut a cross in dough, about 1cm deep. Brush with a little extra buttermilk, then sift a little extra flour over dough. Cook in covered barbecue, using indirect heat, following manufacturer's instructions, about 40 minutes or until cooked.

SERVES 6 TO 8

PEARS WITH RICOTTA, DATE AND MAPLE FILLING

1¹/₄ cups (250g) ricotta cheese
¹/₄ cup (40g) seeded chopped dates
¹/₄ teaspoon ground cinnamon
1 teaspoon sugar
4 medium (920g) pears
¹/₂ cup (125ml) maple syrup
¹/₄ cup (60ml) water

Combine cheese, dates, cinnamon and sugar in small bowl. *[Can be made ahead to this stage. Cover, refrigerate overnight.]*

Cut pears in half lengthways; using a teaspoon, scoop out seeds. Place a heaped tablespoon of cheese mixture in hollow of each pear half. Place pears in disposable baking dish, drizzle with combined maple syrup and water. Cover tightly with greased foil, cook in covered barbecue, using indirect heat, following manufacturer's instructions, 30 minutes or until pears are tender.

SERVES 8

MAPLE APPLES WITH ALMONDS AND MASCARPONE

4 large (800g) apples
¹/₂ cup (125ml) maple syrup
¹/₂ cup (40g) flaked almonds
¹/₄ teaspoon ground cinnamon
2 teaspoons icing sugar mixture
³/₄ cup (180g) mascarpone cheese

Peel and core apples. Place in small disposable baking dish; pour maple syrup over apples. Cook in covered barbecue, using indirect heat, following the

SUGARED BRIOCHE SURPRISES

1 cup (170g) seeded prunes, halved
$1/3$ cup (80ml) brandy
4 x 100g sugared brioche
$3/4$ cup (90g) unroasted chopped
    hazelnuts, toasted
100g dark chocolate,
    chopped roughly
2 tablespoons caster sugar
3 eggs, beaten lightly

Place prunes and brandy in medium bowl. *[Best made ahead to this stage. Cover, refrigerate 3 hours or overnight.]*

Slice tops off each brioche; carefully scoop out and reserve inside crumb, leaving a thin shell. Blend or process reserved crumb until mixture resembles fine breadcrumbs. Combine crumbs and prune mixture in medium bowl with remaining ingredients. Divide prune mixture among brioche; replace tops. Place brioche on wire cake rack in disposable baking dish; cover lightly with foil. Cook in covered barbecue, using indirect heat, following manufacturer's instructions, 10 minutes. Remove foil, cook 2 minutes or until tops are crisp.

MAKES 4

Left, from top Maple apples with almonds and mascarpone; Pears with ricotta, date and maple filling
Below Sugared brioche surprises

manufacturer's instructions, 10 minutes. Turn apples, brush with maple syrup from dish, cook 15 minutes or until tender.

Meanwhile, place almonds on small oven tray, sprinkle with combined cinnamon and icing sugar. Cook in covered barbecue 5 minutes or until almonds and apples are toasted.

Serve apples drizzled with syrup from dish, topped with mascarpone and scattered with almonds.

SERVES 4

Sweet pizzas

We used frozen pizza bases with no savoury ingredients for these recipes. To make your own, use a third of the quantity of the basic dough recipe on page 106.

STRAWBERRY COINTREAU PIZZA WITH MASCARPONE

25cm pizza base
1/4 cup (60ml) strawberry jam
1 tablespoon Cointreau
250g strawberries, halved
1/2 cup (125g) mascarpone cheese
2 teaspoons Cointreau, extra
2 teaspoons icing sugar mixture

Cook pizza base on heated oiled barbecue until browned both sides. Spread with combined jam, liqueur and strawberries. Cook in covered barbecue, using indirect heat, following manufacturer's instructions, about 10 minutes or until base is crisp. Serve topped with combined cheese, extra liqueur and icing sugar.

SERVES 4

BAKED FIG AND DATE RICOTTA PIZZA

25cm pizza base
1 egg yolk
1¼ cups (250g) ricotta cheese
1/2 cup (80g) finely chopped, seeded dates
4 medium (240g) figs, sliced thinly
1 tablespoon brown sugar

Cook pizza base on heated oiled barbecue until browned both sides. Combine egg yolk and cheese in small bowl; stir in dates. Spread mixture over pizza base. Arrange figs over cheese mixture. Sprinkle figs with sugar. Cook pizza in covered barbecue, using indirect heat, following manufacturer's instructions, about 10 minutes or until figs are tender.

SERVES 4

CARDAMOM SPICED APPLE PIZZA

25cm pizza base
4 large (800g) apples, peeled, cored
10 cardamom pods
1/4 cup (60ml) water
20g butter
1 tablespoon caster sugar
70g packaged cream cheese, softened
1 tablespoon cream
2 teaspoons finely chopped palm sugar
1 vanilla bean
1 tablespoon icing sugar mixture

Cook pizza base on heated oiled barbecue until browned both sides. Roughly chop 3 of the apples. Wrap cardamom in muslin. Combine chopped apple, water, butter, cardamom and caster sugar in medium pan. Simmer apple mixture, stirring, until apple is soft and pulpy; discard cardamom pods.

Meanwhile, combine cream cheese, cream, palm sugar and the seeds scraped from the vanilla bean in small bowl. Spread mixture over prepared pizza base; top with apple mixture. Thinly slice remaining apple, arrange overlapping slices on apple mixture; sprinkle with icing sugar. Cook pizza in covered barbecue, using indirect heat, following manufacturer's instructions, about 10 minutes or until apple slices are tender.

SERVES 4

CARAMEL BANANA PIZZA

25cm pizza base
2 small (260g) bananas, sliced

CARAMEL SAUCE
2/3 cup (160ml) cream
1/4 cup (50g) firmly packed brown sugar
1 tablespoon maple syrup
10g butter

Cook pizza base on heated oiled barbecue until browned both sides. Top with Caramel Sauce and banana. Cook in covered barbecue, using manufacturer's instructions about 10 minutes or until bananas are soft and base is crisp.

Caramel Sauce Combine all ingredients in small pan; cook over low heat, without boiling, until sugar dissolves. Bring to boil, simmer, uncovered, until thickened.

SERVES 4

Below, from left Strawberry Cointreau pizza with mascarpone; Baked fig and date ricotta pizza; Cardamon spiced apple pizza; Caramel banana pizza

RHUBARB GINGER SAUCE

3 cups (330g) chopped rhubarb
1/2 cup (110g) caster sugar
1 tablespoon chopped glacé ginger

Combine rhubarb and sugar in medium pan, stir over heat, without boiling, until sugar dissolves. Bring to boil, simmer, uncovered, about 8 minutes or until rhubarb is very soft. Blend or process mixture with ginger until smooth. Serve over ice-cream.

MAKES ABOUT 1 CUP (250ml)

PINEAPPLE COCONUT SAUCE

400g can crushed
**   pineapple, drained**
1/4 cup (60ml) Malibu
300ml cream
1/2 cup (125ml) coconut cream

Blend or process pineapple, Malibu, cream and coconut cream until almost smooth. Serve sauce over ice-cream with toasted flaked coconut, if desired.

MAKES ABOUT 4 CUPS (1 litre)

Above, from left Rocky road sauce; Pineapple coconut sauce; Rhubarb ginger sauce; Summer berry compote; Caramel pistachio sauce; Sticky lemon and passionfruit syrup

CARAMEL PISTACHIO SAUCE

300ml thickened cream
20g butter
1/4 cup (60ml) golden syrup
1/2 cup (100g) firmly packed
**   brown sugar**
1/3 cup (50g) roughly chopped
**   shelled pistachios, toasted**

Combine cream, butter, syrup and sugar in medium pan. Bring to boil, stirring; simmer, uncovered, about 10 minutes or until sauce thickens slightly. Stir in nuts. Serve warm or cold over ice-cream.

MAKES ABOUT 2 CUPS (500ml)

ROCKY ROAD SAUCE

300ml thickened cream
100g dark chocolate, chopped
1/2 cup (100g) marshmallows
2 tablespoons chopped unsalted
**   roasted peanuts**

Combine cream and chocolate in small pan, stir over low heat until chocolate has melted. Add marshmallows and peanuts, stir over low heat until marshmallows have almost melted. Serve warm or cold over ice-cream.

MAKES ABOUT 2 CUPS (500ml)

SUMMER BERRY COMPOTE

300g fresh blueberries
250g fresh raspberries
200g fresh blackberries
1/2 cup (80g) icing sugar mixture

Combine berries in large bowl. Place half the berries and sugar in medium pan over low heat. Cook, uncovered, about 5 minutes or until berries have softened. Blend or process berry mixture until smooth. Stir in remaining berries. Cover; refrigerate 1 hour before serving with cream, yogurt or ice-cream.

MAKES ABOUT 3 CUPS (750ml)

STICKY LEMON AND PASSIONFRUIT SYRUP

3/4 cup (180ml) water
1/4 cup (60ml) lemon juice
3/4 cup (165g) caster sugar
1/3 cup (80 ml) fresh
**   passionfruit pulp**

Combine water, juice and sugar in small pan. Stir over heat, without boiling, until sugar is dissolved. Add passionfruit, bring to boil, simmer, uncovered, until syrup thickens slightly. Serve with ice-cream.

MAKES ABOUT 1 CUP (250ml)

FIGS, HONEYCOMB AND CINNAMON ICE-CREAM

Fresh honeycomb is available from health food stores.

6 medium (360g) figs
500g fresh honeycomb
500ml vanilla ice-cream
2 teaspoons ground cinnamon

Cut figs in half lengthways. Cook on heated oiled barbecue until browned. Cut honeycomb into 2cm strips. Combine ice-cream and cinnamon. Serve figs with honeycomb and cinnamon ice-cream.

SERVES 4 TO 6

CARAMELISED PEACHES WITH SPICED YOGURT

6 medium (1.2kg) peaches, peeled, halved
1/4 cup (50g) firmly packed brown sugar

SPICED YOGURT
200ml yogurt
1/4 teaspoon ground cinnamon
1/4 teaspoon ground cardamom

Cook prepared peaches on heated oiled barbecue griddle plate until browned; sprinkle with sugar, cook, turning, until sugar dissolves and starts to bubble. Serve with Spiced Yogurt.

Spiced Yogurt Combine all ingredients in small bowl.

SERVES 4

ROCKET PESTO AND PARMESAN TURKISH BREAD

1/4 cup (40g) pine nuts, toasted
50g rocket leaves
1 clove garlic, crushed
1/4 cup (20g) finely grated
    parmesan cheese
1/4 cup (60ml) light olive oil
100g parmesan cheese, extra
40cm long Turkish bread

Blend or process pine nuts, rocket, garlic and grated cheese until almost smooth. With motor operating gradually pour in oil. [Can be made ahead to this stage. Cover, refrigerate overnight.]

Using a vegetable peeler shave extra cheese into thin strips.

Place bread on oven tray, spread top with pesto, sprinkle with shaved cheese. Cook in covered barbecue, using indirect heat, following manufacturer's instructions, about 10 minutes or until cheese melts and is browned lightly.

SERVES 4

OLIVE TAPENADE AND MOZZARELLA TURKISH BREAD

2/3 cup (80g) seeded black olives
2 tablespoons coarsely chopped
    fresh parsley
2 teaspoons grated lemon rind
1 tablespoon lemon juice
1 clove garlic, crushed
2 tablespoons drained capers
40cm long Turkish bread
250g mozzarella cheese,
    sliced thinly

Blend or process olives, parsley, rind, juice, garlic and capers until almost smooth. [Can be made ahead. Cover, refrigerate overnight.]

Place bread on oven tray, spread top with olive tapenade, top with cheese. Cook in covered barbecue, using indirect heat, following manufacturer's instructions, about 10 minutes or until cheese melts and is browned lightly.

SERVES 4

TURKISH BREAD WITH SUN-DRIED TOMATO BUTTER

100g butter, softened
2 tablespoons finely chopped
    drained sun-dried tomatoes
1 tablespoon finely chopped fresh
    basil leaves
2 x 15cm rounds Turkish bread

Combine butter, tomato and basil in small bowl. [Can be made ahead. Cover, refrigerate overnight.]

Split Turkish bread in half, cut each half into 3 pieces. Cook bread on heated oiled barbecue until browned both sides. Spread with sun-dried tomato butter.

SERVES 4

TURKISH BREAD WITH GARLIC AND CHIVE BUTTER

4 cloves garlic
100g butter, softened
1 tablespoon finely chopped
    fresh chives
2 x 15cm rounds Turkish bread

Place unpeeled garlic in dry heavy-based pan, cook over low heat until browned all over; remove skin.

Combine butter, chives and finely chopped garlic in small bowl. [Can be made ahead. Cover, refrigerate overnight.]

Split Turkish bread in half. Cut each half into 3 pieces. Cook bread on heated oiled barbecue until browned both sides. Spread with garlic and chive butter.

SERVES 4

Left, from top Figs, honeycomb and cinnamon ice-cream; Caramelised peaches with spiced yogurt
Right, clockwise from top left Rocket pesto and parmesan Turkish bread; Olive tapenade and mozzarella Turkish bread; Turkish bread with sun-dried tomato butter; Turkish bread with garlic and chive butter

Wooden tray from Corso de' Fiori

DATE DUMPLINGS IN BUTTERSCOTCH SAUCE

1/3 cup (55g) seeded chopped dates
2 tablespoons boiling water
1 1/4 cups (175g) self-raising flour
30g butter, chopped
1/2 cup (125ml) milk, approximately

BUTTERSCOTCH SAUCE
3/4 cup (150g) firmly packed brown sugar
150g butter, chopped
3/4 cup (180ml) cream

Combine dates and the water in small bowl; stand 10 minutes or until dates are soft. Place flour in medium bowl; rub in butter. Add undrained date mixture and enough milk to mix to a soft, sticky dough. Pour hot Butterscotch Sauce into 2.5 litre (10-cup capacity) ovenproof dish or 26cm x 36cm disposable baking dish. Drop tablespoons of dumpling mixture into sauce. Cover dish, cook in covered barbecue, using indirect heat, following manufacturer's instructions, 15 minutes or until dumplings are firm.

Butterscotch Sauce Combine all ingredients in medium pan; stir over heat, without boiling, until sugar dissolves. Simmer, without stirring, 3 minutes.

SERVES 4 TO 6

RASPBERRY PECAN BREAD-AND-BUTTER PUDDING

10 slices raisin bread
40g butter, softened
150g raspberries
3 eggs
1/4 cup (55g) caster sugar
2 1/2 cups (625ml) milk
1 teaspoon vanilla essence
1/2 cup (60g) chopped pecans
2 tablespoons brown sugar
2 tablespoons golden syrup

Trim crusts from bread, spread both sides of bread with butter, cut each slice into 4 triangles. Arrange bread in two 13cm x 18cm (4-cup capacity) ovenproof dishes or disposable baking dishes, sprinkle with raspberries. Whisk eggs, caster sugar, milk and essence in large jug; pour over bread. Sprinkle with combined nuts and brown sugar. Cook puddings in covered barbecue, using indirect heat, following manufacturer's instructions, 45 minutes or until custard has set. Serve puddings drizzled with golden syrup.

SERVES 4

BASIC PIZZA DOUGH

Each of the following toppings is enough for one quantity of this Basic Pizza Dough. Cook base in covered barbecue, using indirect heat, following manufacturer's instructions, 5 minutes, then turn dough over before covering with topping. If you don't want to make your own pizza dough, there are many ready-made pizza bases on the market.

1 1/2 teaspoons (7g) yeast
1 cup (250ml) warm water
2 teaspoons sugar
3 cups (450g) plain flour
1 teaspoon salt

Whisk yeast, water and sugar in small bowl; cover, stand in warm place about 10 minutes or until mixture is frothy. Sift flour and salt into large bowl, stir in yeast mixture; mix to a soft dough. Knead dough on floured surface about 10 minutes or until smooth. Place dough in large oiled bowl; cover, stand in warm place about 1 hour or until dough is doubled in size.

To make mini pizzas, divide dough into 8 portions, roll each portion into a 15cm round. To make plate-size pizzas, divide dough into 4 portions, roll each portion into a 25cm round. Cook dough on grill, in covered barbecue, using indirect heat, following manufacturer's instructions, 5 minutes (dough may puff up; if it does, flatten, allowing air to escape). Turn dough over. Cover with any of the following toppings.

SERVES 4 TO 8

CHORIZO PIZZA

1/3 cup (80ml) bottled pasta sauce
2 (260g) chorizo sausages, sliced
1 medium (150g) white
 onion, sliced
1 medium (200g) red capsicum,
 sliced
1/2 cup (60g) seeded black
 olives, sliced
2 tablespoons chopped fresh
 basil leaves
200g bocconcini cheese, sliced

Spread cooked pizza base with sauce, top with sausage, onion, capsicum, olives, basil and bocconcini. Cook in covered barbecue, using indirect heat, following manufacturer's instructions, about 10 minutes or until cheese has melted.

ROASTED VEGETABLE PIZZA

4 (240g) baby eggplant, sliced
3 medium (360g) zucchini, sliced
1/2 cup (125ml) sun-dried
 tomato pesto
1 medium (200g) red capsicum,
 seeded, chopped
200g haloumi cheese, sliced

Cook eggplant and zucchini on heated oiled barbecue until just tender. Spread cooked pizza base with pesto, top with eggplant, zucchini, capsicum and cheese. Cook in covered barbecue, using indirect heat, following manufacturer's instructions, about 10 minutes or until cheese has melted.

THREE-MUSHROOM PIZZA

20g butter, melted
1 clove garlic, crushed
100g button mushrooms, sliced
100g Swiss brown
 mushrooms, sliced
100g oyster mushrooms, halved
1/2 cup (60g) coarsely grated
 smoked cheddar cheese
1/2 cup (40g) finely grated
 parmesan cheese
1 cup (125g) coarsely grated
 cheddar cheese

Brush cooked pizza base with combined butter and garlic, top with mushrooms and cheese. Cook in covered barbecue, using indirect heat, following manufacturer's instructions, about 10 minutes or until cheese has melted.

SATAY PRAWN PIZZA

1/2 cup (125ml) bottled
 satay marinade
1 medium (150g) brown
 onion, sliced
100g snow peas, sliced thinly
500g small uncooked
 prawns, shelled
1/2 cup (75g) roasted cashews
2 tablespoons chopped fresh
 coriander leaves
1 cup (125g) pizza cheese

Spread cooked pizza base with satay marinade, top with onion, snow peas, prawns, cashews, coriander and cheese. Cook in covered barbecue, using indirect heat, following manufacturer's instructions, about 10 minutes or until cheese has melted.

Left, from top Date dumplings in butterscotch sauce; Raspberry pecan bread-and-butter pudding
Above, clockwise from top left Chorizo pizza; Three-mushroom pizza; Roasted vegetable pizza; Satay prawn pizza

Menu suggestions

Although many barbecues are spontaneous events, a little planning can result in a superlative meal. Choose salads and other accompaniments according to your preferences and the season. As the number of servings in each recipe may vary, please adjust quantities to cover the numbers you're feeding.

THE NEW AUSTRALIAN CUISINE

Balsamic-flavoured octopus

Tomato and bocconcini lamb stacks

Pumpkin and walnut damper

Maple apples with almonds and mascarpone

A day ahead: Clean and marinate octopus; toast almonds for maple apples.

3 hours ahead: Cook and mash pumpkin for damper.

OH CALCUTTA!

Indian spiced beef with dhal

Tandoori chicken with cucumber mint raita

Indian chutney

Fresh fruit

Up to 1 week ahead: Make Indian chutney.

A day ahead: Prepare Indian spiced beef; marinate chicken in tandoori mixture.

3 hours ahead: Make cucumber and mint raita; soak smoking chips in wine.

1 hour ahead: Make dhal.

THE SPICE IS RIGHT

Tuna with coriander pesto

Indian spiced lamb with aloo chop

Spiced yogurt

A day ahead: Marinate lamb; make coriander pesto.

3 hours ahead: Prepare both aloo chop and yogurt mixtures.

IMPRESSING THE IN-LAWS

Crab and prawn cakes with sweet chilli cucumber salsa

Chicken with caramelised pear

Baby bok choy with red onion and balsamic jam

Char-grilled fruits

A day ahead: Make crab and prawn cakes (or make ahead and freeze); slice and flatten chicken, refrigerate between layers of plastic wrap; make red onion and balsamic jam.

3 hours ahead: Make sweet chilli cucumber salsa; prepare fruits for grilling; make passionfruit syrup.

AN AEGEAN MEDLEY

Lemon and mustard calamari

Greek-style beef with tzatziki and salad

Baked fig and date ricotta pizza

A day ahead: Make calamari seasoning mixture and its lemon and mustard dressing; marinate beef and make dressing for its salad.

3 hours ahead: Fill calamari hoods with seasoning; make tzatziki; prepare ricotta mixture for pizza.

LIGHT AND YUMMY

Grilled spatchcock with citrus flavours

Mesclun and tomatoes with Robby's dressing

Figs, honeycomb and cinnamon ice-cream

A day ahead: Marinate spatchcock; make Robby's dressing; combine cinnamon and ice-cream then refreeze.

Above Mustard honey glazed vegetables, page 92

IN THE FRENCH MANNER

Redcurrant-glazed duck

Mustard honey glazed vegetables

Sugared brioche surprises

A day ahead: Make glazes for duck and vegetables; combine prunes and brandy for brioche.

3 hours ahead: Fill brioche.

PAC-RIM EXTRAVAGANZA

Balsamic and ginger beef

Lemon grass and chilli-smoked swordfish

Mixed vegetables

Ice-cream with rhubarb ginger sauce

A day ahead: Marinate both beef and fish, separately; make rhubarb ginger sauce.

1 hour ahead: Prepare vegetables and cumin mixture.

SEASIDE SEAFEAST

Tunisian prawns with coriander potatoes

Sardines in chermoulla with tomato salsa

Seafood brochettes with lime and coconut

Char-grilled vegetables

A day ahead: Marinate prawns and fish for brochettes; make coriander mixture and chermoulla; toast pistachios.

3 hours ahead: Combine sardines with chermoulla; coat prawns with pistachios; make tomato salsa.

Above Chicken with caramelised pear, page 34

AFTER-CRICKET FEAST

Sausages with garlic mushrooms

Sweet chilli beef ribs

Damper

Tomatoes with fetta, olives and polenta

Caramel banana pizza

A day ahead: Marinate sweet chilli beef ribs; make fetta mixture for tomatoes; make caramel sauce for pizza.

1 hour ahead: Make garlic mushrooms.

THE MEXICAN WAVE

Beef fajitas

Tex-Mex ribs with corn muffins

Nachos sausages

A day ahead: Marinate both the beef and ribs, separately.

3 hours ahead: Wrap tortillas in foil; make salsa to accompany fajitas; prepare vegetables for corn muffins.

TEENAGER'S BIRTHDAY

Sausages with maple syrup and mustard

Mega beef burgers

Ice-cream or fresh fruit with rocky road sauce

A day ahead: Make beef patties (or make ahead and freeze).

3 hours ahead: Make the rocky road sauce.

LA DOLCE VITA

Garlic and rosemary smoked lamb

Three-mushroom pizza

Rocket and parmesan salad with Italian dressing

A day ahead: Prepare lamb; mix Italian dressing; grate cheeses for pizza.

3 hours ahead: Soak smoking chips in cold water.

Just before serving: Make salad by tossing rocket leaves with Italian dressing; top with shaved parmesan.

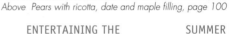
Above Pears with ricotta, date and maple filling, page 100

ENTERTAINING THE NEIGHBOURS

Pork steaks with caraway and cabbage

Roasted beetroot

Pears with ricotta, date and maple filling

A day ahead: Combine date and ricotta mixture for the pears.

FEEDING GOOD FRIENDS

Roasted whole chicken with caramelised lemon

Corn with sage and bacon

Peppered spinach and fetta damper

Fresh or barbecued fruit

A day ahead: Prepare corn; soak in combined milk and water.

3 hours ahead: Prepare chicken; press sage and bacon onto corn and tie husks.

AN INDIAN BANQUET

Barbecued lamb chops with raita

Chicken tikka with grilled bananas

Cardamom spiced apple pizza

A day ahead: Marinate chicken; make coconut mixture for bananas; prepare apple and cream cheese mixture for pizza.

3 hours ahead: Make raita.

SUMMER IN THE CITY

Apricot-seasoned chicken

Green salad with honey Dijon dressing

Yogurt with summer berry compote

A day ahead: Make seasoning for chicken; make honey Dijon salad dressing; prepare summer berry compote.

3 hours ahead: Roll up apricot-seasoned chicken.

DOWN AT THE BEACH

Lime chicken on lemon grass skewers

Asian-style snapper in banana leaves

Char-grilled fruits

A day ahead: Skewer chicken onto lemon grass and marinate. Make lime and macadamia dressing for chicken skewers.

3 hours ahead: Prepare and wrap snapper in banana leaves; prepare fruit and make syrup.

NEW YEAR'S BRUNCH

Seafood platter

Tossed salad with French dressing

Ice-cream with caramel pistachio sauce

A day ahead: Clean and marinate seafood; make the French salad dressing; make caramel pistachio sauce.

Above Beef fajitas, page 12

Above Butterflied hot and sour prawns, page 78

SOME LIKE IT HOT

**Butterflied hot and
sour prawns**

**Ginger pork with mango
and red onion salsa**

**Fresh or barbecued fruit
with pineapple
coconut sauce**

A day ahead: Prepare and
marinate prawns; marinate
pork; prepare pineapple
coconut sauce.

JAPANESE HIGHLIGHTS

**Ginger tuna with
wasabi drizzle**

**Teriyaki snapper
with soba**

**Steamed rice and
barbecued asparagus**

A day ahead: Marinate tuna and
snapper; make wasabi drizzle.

ONLY VEGETARIANS ALLOWED

**Baked ricotta with
char-grilled vegetables**

**Mixed seed
beer bread**

**Curly endive and watercress
with Russian dressing**

A day ahead: Prepare and
measure all seeds for bread for
damper; make Russian dressing.

TAKE ME TO THE KASBAH

**Quail grilled
North-African style**

**Lemon and artichoke rack
of lamb**

Garlic chilli potato kebabs

3 hours ahead: Make seasoning
and cumin dressing for quail;
soak skewers; season quail;
cook potatoes for kebabs.

A SPECIAL OCCASION

**Standing rib roast
provençal**

Orange glazed ham

**Turkey with raisin and
Brazil nut seasoning**

**Potatoes with raclette
cheese and garlic**

**Raspberry pecan bread-
and-butter pudding**

A day ahead: Marinate beef;
make seasoning for turkey;
prepare orange glaze for ham.

3 hours ahead: Season and tie
turkey; wrap potatoes and
garlic in foil.

THAI-TANIC

Thai beef salad

**Snapper filled with
Thai-style vegetables**

Coriander potatoes

A day ahead: Marinate beef;
mix Thai dressing; prepare
coriander mixture for potatoes.

WHEN THE BOSS COMES
TO DINNER

**Duck with Madeira and
juniper berries**

**Sugar and rosemary
smoked rump**

**Mixed leaf salad with
thousand island dressing**

**Strawberry Cointreau pizza
with mascarpone**

A day ahead: Marinate duck;
make thousand island dressing;
combine mascarpone with sugar
and Cointreau for pizza.

AN AMERICAN PICNIC

**Sticky ribs with Boston
baked beans**

Corn on the cob

**Baby cos lettuce with
Caesar dressing**

Boston brown bread

A day ahead: Soak beans;
prepare and soak corn;
marinate ribs; make Caesar
salad dressing.

Above Thai beef salad, page 29

SOMETHING OLD,
SOMETHING NEW

Burgers bellissimo

Jazzy beef sausages

**Ice-cream with sticky
lemon and
passionfruit syrup**

A day ahead: Make burger
patties (or can be made earlier
and frozen); make sauce for
sausages; make sticky lemon
and passionfruit syrup.

THE EMPIRE STRIKES BACK

**Vodka and Sichuan pepper
glazed chicken**

**Shredded red cabbage with
Russian dressing**

**Date dumplings in
butterscotch sauce**

A day ahead: Make glaze for
chicken and Russian dressing.

1 hour ahead: Prepare blini
mixture to accompany chicken;
make butterscotch sauce.

Catering for crowds

*Here we have given beverage quantity guidelines when
catering for large crowds.*

750ml bottle beer	= 3 to 4 200ml glasses
750ml bottle Champagne	= 6 x 125ml flutes
750ml bottle wine	= 5 x 150ml glasses
4-litre wine cask	= 26 x 150ml glasses
750ml bottle spirits	= 15 x 50ml nips
5-litre cask orange juice	= 20 x 250ml glasses
10 fresh oranges	= 6 x 200ml glasses
375ml can soft drink	= 2 x 200ml glasses
1.25-litre bottle soft drink	= 6 x 200ml glasses
250g tea	= 80 cups
100g instant coffee	= 65 cups
200g ground coffee	= 40 cups
3 litres water	= 25 cups
1 litre milk	= 40 cups
200g drinking chocolate	= 22 cups

10kg ice will chill about 24 bottles of wine or about 48 small bottles of beer.

FLAVOURS FROM THE
SPICE ISLANDS

**Blackened blue eye
with sweet tomato relish**

**Sumac lamb roasts with
citrus tabbouleh**

**Caramelised peaches with
spiced yogurt**

Up to 1 week ahead: Make
sweet tomato relish.

A day ahead: Marinate fish and
lamb; make spicy mixture for
fish; make spiced yogurt.

Above Sumac lamb roasts with citrus tabbouleh, page 48

Meat cuts suitable for barbecuing

BEEF
DIRECT HEAT: rib eye steak *(scotch fillet)*
fillet steak
rump steak
rib steak *(with bone-in)*
T-bone steak
boneless sirloin steak *(New York cut)*
sirloin steak with bone in *(porterhouse)*
oyster blade steak
blade steak *(with and without bone)*
silverside minute steak
topside steak

INDIRECT HEAT: topside roast
blade roast
silverside roast
standing rib roast
sirloin roast
rib eye roast
rump roast
butt fillet *(beef fillet from the rump)*
eye fillet
ribs

LAMB
DIRECT HEAT: cutlets
diced lamb *(for kebabs)*
eye of loin
chump chop
loin chop
forequarter chop
fillet

INDIRECT HEAT: boned loin
boned shoulder
crown roast
mini roast *(round or topside)*
rack
leg
tunnel-boned leg
butterfly leg
four-rib roast
party rack
lamb shank
lamb drumstick
neck fillet roast

VEAL
DIRECT HEAT: fillet steak
rump steak
shoulder steak
leg steak
forequarter chops
leg chops
loin chops
eye of loin
eye fillet medallion
cutlets

INDIRECT HEAT: shoulder
fillet
leg
loin *(bone-in)*
rump

PORK
DIRECT HEAT: loin chop
forequarter chop
loin steak
rump steak
leg steak
loin medallion steak
midloin butterfly steak
scotch steak
diced *(for kebabs)*
spareribs
loin cutlets

INDIRECT HEAT: leg
topside
rolled shoulder
silverside
rack
loin
rump mini roast
scotch *(neck)*
boneless loin
ribs
tenderloin

ALL-PURPOSE SEASONING a commercial seasoning consisting of salt, paprika, onion, herbs, spices and black pepper.

BACON RASHERS also known as slices of bacon; made from pork side, cured and smoked. **Streaky bacon** is the fatty end of a bacon rasher (slice), without the lean (eye) meat.

BAKING POWDER a raising agent consisting mainly of 2 parts cream of tartar to 1 part bicarbonate of soda (baking soda).

BARBECUE SAUCE a spicy, tomato-based sauce used to marinate, baste or as an accompaniment.

BEANS
Black, also known as turtle beans or black kidney beans, are an earthy-flavoured dried bean completely different from the better-known Chinese black beans (which are fermented soy beans). Most used in Mexican, South and Central American and Caribbean cooking, especially for soups and stews.
Black-eyed also known as black-eyed peas. (Usually purchased dried.)

BICARBONATE OF SODA also known as baking soda.

BREADCRUMBS
Stale 1- or 2-day-old bread made into crumbs by grating, blending or processing.

horseradish

BRIOCHE rich French yeast bread made with butter and eggs. It is available from French bakeries or some of the better breadshops.

BURGHUL also known as bulghur wheat; hulled steamed wheat kernels that, once dried, are crushed into various sized grains. Used in Middle-Eastern dishes, such as kibbeh and taboulleh.

BUTTER use salted or unsalted ("sweet") butter; a stick of butter equals 125g.

BUTTERMILK low-fat milk, cultured to give a slightly sour, tangy taste; low-fat yogurt can be substituted.

CAPSICUM also known as bell pepper or, simply, pepper. Seeds and pithy membrane should be discarded before use.

CHEESE
Bocconcini small rounds of fresh "baby" mozzarella, a delicate, semi-soft, white cheese traditionally made in Italy from buffalo milk. Spoils rapidly so must be kept under refrigeration, in brine, for no more than 1 or 2 days.
Fetta Greek in origin; a crumbly textured goat or sheep milk cheese with a sharp, salty taste.
Haloumi a firm, cream-coloured sheep milk cheese matured in brine; somewhat like a minty, salty fetta in flavour, haloumi can be grilled or fried, briefly, without breaking down.
Mascarpone a fresh, thick, triple-cream cheese with a delicately sweet, slightly sour taste.
Mozzarella a semi-soft cheese with a delicate, fresh taste; has a low melting point and stringy texture when heated.
Parmesan a sharp-tasting, dry, hard cheese, made from skim or part-skim milk and aged for at

least a year before being sold. Parmigiano Reggiano, from Italy, aged a minimum of three years, is one of the best.
Pecorino hard, dry, yellow cheese, which has a sharp pungent taste. Originally from sheep milk, now made with cow milk. If unavailable, use parmesan.
Pizza Cheese a commercial blend of varying proportions of processed grated cheddar, mozzarella and parmesan.
Raclette is the generic name of a semi-hard cheese, which is gold in colour with a few small holes and a rough light brown rind. It has a distinct nutty flavour and melts well.
Ricotta a sweet, fairly moist, fresh curd cheese with a low fat content.

CHILLIES available in many types and sizes. Generally, the smaller the chilli the hotter it is. Use rubber gloves when seeding and chopping fresh chillies as they can burn your skin. Removing membranes and seeds reduces the heat level.
Flakes crushed dried chillies.
Powder the Asian variety is the hottest, made from ground chillies; it can be used as a substitute for fresh chillies in the proportion of 1/2 teaspoon ground chilli powder to 1 medium chopped fresh chilli.
Sweet Chilli Sauce is a comparatively mild, Thai-type sauce made from red chillies, sugar, garlic and vinegar.

CHOY SUM also known as flowering bok choy or flowering white cabbage.

COCONUT
Cream produced by squeezing the coconut flesh. Available in cans at most supermarkets.
Flaked dried flaked coconut flesh available in packets.
Milk available in cans and cartons; made from coconut and water.

COUSCOUS a fine, grain-like cereal product, originally from North Africa; made from semolina.

CREAM
Fresh (minimum fat content 35%) also known as pure cream and pouring cream; has no additives, unlike commercially thickened cream, which uses gelatine.
Light sour (minimum fat content 18%) cream specifically cultured to produce its characteristic tart flavour. Because it is thinner than normal sour cream, it should not be substituted for sour cream in cooking – the consistency will affect recipe results.
Sour (minimum fat content 35%) a thick, commercially cultured soured cream good for dips, toppings and baked cheesecakes.
Thickened (minimum fat content 35%) a whipping cream containing a thickener such as gelatine.

CREME FRAICHE (minimum fat content 35%: not low in fat as many believe) velvety texture and tangy taste; available in cartons from delicatessens and super-markets. To make creme fraiche, combine 300ml cream with 300ml sour cream in bowl; cover, stand at room temperature until mixture is thick; this will take 1 or 2 days, depending on room temperature. Refrigerate before using. Makes about 2 1/2 cups (625ml).

CURRY
Red paste commercial versions consist of chilli, onion, garlic, oil, lemon rind, shrimp paste, cumin, paprika, turmeric and pepper. Red paste is hotter than green paste.
Tandoori paste Indian blend of fragrant spices, including turmeric, paprika, chilli powder, saffron, cardamom and garam masala.

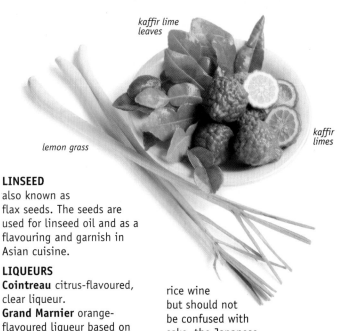

kaffir lime leaves

lemon grass

kaffir limes

Tikka paste consists of chilli, coriander, cumin, lentil flour, garlic, ginger, oil, turmeric, fennel, pepper, cloves, cinnamon and cardamom.

EGGPLANT also known as aubergine.

ESSENCES also known as extracts; the byproduct of distillation of plants. Try to buy pure essences.

FISH SAUCE also called nam pla or nuoc nam; made from pulverised salted fermented fish, most often anchovies. Has a pungent smell and strong taste; use sparingly. There are many kinds, of varying intensity.

FLOUR
Plain an all-purpose flour, made from wheat.
Self-raising plain flour sifted with baking powder in the proportion of 1 cup flour to 2 level teaspoons baking powder.
Rye flour milled from rye.
Wholemeal plain also known as all-purpose wholewheat flour, has no baking powder added.

GARAM MASALA a blend of spices, originating in northern India; based on varying proportions of cardamom, cinnamon, cloves, coriander, fennel and cumin, roasted and ground together. Black pepper and chilli can be added for a hotter version.

GINGER
Fresh also known as green or root ginger; the gnarled root of a tropical plant. Can be kept, peeled and covered with dry sherry in a jar and refrigerated, or it can be stored, peeled and frozen, in an airtight container.

GOLDEN SYRUP a byproduct of refined sugarcane; pure maple syrup or honey can be substituted.

GREEN GINGER WINE alcoholic sweet wine infused with finely ground ginger.

HERBS we used dried (not ground) herbs. If you need to substitute dried for fresh herbs, use in the proportion of 1:4 for fresh herbs; eg, 1 teaspoon dried herbs equals 4 teaspoons (1 tablespoon) chopped fresh herbs.

HOISIN SAUCE a thick, sweet and spicy Chinese paste made from salted fermented soy beans, onions and garlic; used as a marinade or baste, or to accent stir-fries and barbecued or roasted foods.

HORSERADISH CREAM a creamy prepared paste of grated horseradish, vinegar, oil and sugar.

HORSERADISH, FRESH a plant of the mustard family, with a large white root that has a hot, sharp, pungent flavour. The root is often peeled and grated and used as a condiment.

JUNIPER BERRIES dried berries of an evergreen tree used, on occasion, to flavour savoury dishes.

KAFFIR LIME a medium-sized citrus fruit with wrinkly green skin. The sharp aromatic citrus-flavoured fruit is commonly used in Thai cooking.

KAFFIR LIME LEAVES aromatic leaves of a small citrus tree bearing a wrinkle-skinned yellow-green fruit originally grown in South Africa and Southeast Asia. Used fresh or dried in many Asian dishes.

KIWI FRUIT also known as Chinese gooseberry.

KUMARA Polynesian name of orange-fleshed sweet potato often confused with yam.

LEMON GRASS a tall, sharp-edged grass, lemon-smelling and tasting; the white lower part of each stem is pounded or chopped finely and used in Asian cooking or to infuse as a tea.

LINSEED also known as flax seeds. The seeds are used for linseed oil and as a flavouring and garnish in Asian cuisine.

LIQUEURS
Cointreau citrus-flavoured, clear liqueur.
Grand Marnier orange-flavoured liqueur based on Cognac-brandy.
Pernod aniseed-flavoured liqueur.

MALIBU coconut-flavoured rum-based liquor.

MAPLE SYRUP distilled sap of the sugar maple tree. Maple-Flavoured Syrup or pancake syrup is made from cane sugar and artificial maple flavouring and is not an adequate substitute for the real thing.

MESCLUN often sold as mixed small leaves for salad, and consists of an assortment of edible greens and flowers.

MILK we used full-cream homogenised milk, unless otherwise specified.

MINCE MEAT also known as ground meat, as in beef, pork, lamb and veal.

MIRIN a sweet, low-alcohol rice wine used in Japanese cooking; sometimes referred to simply as rice wine but should not be confused with sake, the Japanese rice wine made for drinking.

MIXED SPICE a blend of ground spices usually consisting of cinnamon, allspice and nutmeg.

MOLASSES a thick, dark brown syrup, the residue after sugar refinement.

MUSHROOMS
Button small, cultivated white mushrooms with a delicate, subtle flavour.
Enoki slender 10cm long body with a tiny head, it is creamy-yellow in colour and crisp in texture. Sold in clumps, it has a mild flavour and is good in stir-fries.
Oyster (abalone) grey-white mushroom shaped like a fan.
Shiitake used mainly in Chinese and Japanese cooking.
Swiss Brown light to dark brown mushrooms with full-bodied flavour. Button or cup mushrooms can be substituted for Swiss browns.

shiitake mushrooms

enoki mushrooms

swiss brown mushrooms

button mushrooms

oyster mushrooms

kiwi fruit

passionfruit

OILS

Olive mono-unsaturated; made from the pressing of tree-ripened olives. Especially good for everyday cooking and as an ingredient in salad dressings.
Extra virgin and virgin the highest quality olive oils, obtained from the first pressing of the olives.
Extra Light or Light describes the mild flavour, not the fat levels.
Peanut pressed from ground peanuts; most commonly used oil in Asian cooking because its high smoke point makes it more suitable.
Sesame made from roasted, crushed, white sesame seeds; used as a flavouring rather than a cooking medium.
Vegetable any of a number of oils sourced from plants rather than animal fats.

ONION

Brown and White are interchangeable. Known as maincrop onions they are recognised by their skin colour. Their pungent moist flesh (varying in colour from white to purple) is very versatile and adds flavour to a vast range of dishes.
Green also known as scallion or (incorrectly) shallot; an immature onion picked before the bulb has formed, having a long, bright-green edible stalk.
Red also known as Spanish, red Spanish or Bermuda onion; a sweet-flavoured, large, purple-red onion that is particularly good eaten raw in salads.
Spring has crisp, narrow green-leafed top and a fairly large sweet white bulb.

ORANGE, BLOOD a medium-sized orange with red or red streaked flesh. It has a sweet flavour.

OYSTER SAUCE Asian in origin, this rich brown sauce is made from oysters and their brine cooked with salt and soy sauce and thickened with starches.

PANCETTA an Italian salt-cured pork roll, usually cut from the belly; used chopped in cooked dishes to add flavour. Bacon can be substituted in most recipes.

PAPRIKA ground dried red capsicum (bell pepper), available sweet or hot.

red onion

brown onion

white onion

spring onion

green onion

PASSIONFRUIT also known as granadilla; a small tropical fruit, native to Brazil, with a tough outer skin surrounding sweet-sour pulp and edible black seeds.

PASTA SAUCE, BOTTLED a prepared tomato-based sauce (sometimes called ragu or sugo on the label); comes in varying degrees of thickness using different spices to alter the flavour.

PINE NUT also known as pignoli; small, cream-coloured kernels obtained from the cones of different varieties of pine trees.

POLENTA a flour-like cereal made of ground corn (maize); similar to cornmeal but coarser and darker in colour; also the name of the dish made from it.

POTATO
Kipfler small and finger-shaped; it has a nutty flavour, and is great baked and used in salads.
New not a variety but an early harvest with a thin, pale skin that's easily rubbed off. Good steamed, and eaten hot or cold in salads.
Pink eye small with off-white skin and deep purple eyes; good steamed, boiled and baked.

PROSCIUTTO salted-cured, air-dried (unsmoked), pressed ham; usually sold in paper-thin slices, ready to eat. Short storage time.

PUMPKIN, NUGGET also called Golden Nugget. Very small, round, orange skin and dark yellow flesh; great baked filled with a variety of seasonings.

REDCURRANT JELLY a preserve made from redcurrants used as a glaze for desserts and meats or in sauces.

RICE
Basmati a fragrant, long-grained white rice. It should be washed several times to remove grit before cooking.
Short-grain (more correctly called medium-grain) fat, almost round grain with a high starch content; tends to clump together when cooked. Ideal for seasonings.
White & wild rice blend pre-packaged blend of white and wild rice. Available from supermarkets and specialty food stores.

RICE WINE a sweet, gold-coloured, low-alcohol wine made from fermented rice.

ROCKET also arugula, rugula and rucola; a green salad leaf.

SAKE Japan's favourite rice wine, used in cooking, marinating and as part of dipping sauces. If sake is unavailable, dry sherry, vermouth or brandy can be used as a substitute. When consumed as a drink, it is served warm. To do this, stand the container in hot water for about 20 minutes to warm the sake.

SATAY MARINADE (bottled) a commercially bottled satay sauce. Generally available.

SAUSAGE
Casing Can be purchased from most butchers.
Chorizo Spanish in origin, a highly seasoned, spicy salami made from ground pork, garlic and red peppers.

SEAFOOD
Balmain bugs also known as shovelnosed lobster. Orange/red coloured crustacean that grows to about 10cm to 20cm.
Blue eye fillets also known as deep sea trevalla or trevally and blue eye cod; thick, moist, white-fleshed.
Boneless fish fillets also known as flake; fish pieces that have been skinned with all bones removed.
Bream also known as yellowfin bream, surf bream and black bream; white flesh with firm fine texture.
Calamari a type of squid.
Garfish also known as piper and halfbeak; small, elongated fish with fine texture, sweet delicate flavour and small soft bones.
Lobster sometimes incorrectly called crayfish. The most common varieties are rock lobster and spiny lobster. Sweet flesh.
Ocean trout a farmed fish with pink, soft flesh, it is from the same family as the Atlantic salmon.
Octopus a member of the cephalopod mollusc family. Has a soft oval shaped body and tentacles without any internal shell or "quill". The skin is grey when raw, turning purple/pink when it is cooked.
Prawns also called shrimp.
Salmon fish with red-pink

firm flesh; moist delicate flavour; few bones.

Sardine small silvery fish with soft, oily flesh.

Scallops bivalve mollusc with fluted shell valve. We used scallops still having the coral (roe) attached.

Small black mussels we used the common variety, known as blue mussels.

Snapper small, firm-fleshed, distinctly flavoured fish sold whole, good for any kind of cooking method; a number of varieties include red, pink and yellowtail snapper.

Sword fish mild-flavoured, firm-fleshed large fish.

Tuna reddish, firm flesh; slightly dry, no bones.

SHALLOTS, also called French shallots, golden shallots or eshalots. Small, elongated, brown-skinned members of the onion family. Grows in tight clusters like garlic.

SICHUAN PEPPER (also known as Chinese pepper) small, red-brown aromatic seeds resembling black peppercorns; they have a peppery-lemon flavour.

SNOW PEAS also called *mange tout* ("eat all").

SOY SAUCE made from fermented soy beans. Several variations are available in most supermarkets and Asian food stores.
Dark used for colour as well as flavour, we used dark soy sauce of Japanese origin.
Light as the name indicates, light in colour. We used a light soy sauce of Japanese origin; generally quite salty.

SPATCHCOCK a small chicken (poussin), no more than 6 weeks old, weighing a maximum 500g. Also, a cooking technique where a small chicken is split open, then flattened and grilled.

SPINACH
English correct name for spinach; delicate, green leaves on thin stems; high in iron, it's good eaten raw or steamed. The green vegetable often called

spinach is correctly known as Swiss chard, silverbeet or seakale.
Silverbeet steam green leafy parts and use as required in recipes.

SPROUTS
Bean also known as bean shoots; tender new growth of assorted beans and seeds germinated for consumption as sprouts. The most readily available are mung bean, soy bean, alfalfa and snow pea sprouts.

STAR ANISE a dried star-shaped pod whose seeds have an astringent aniseed flavour. Used in Asian recipes.

STOCK crumble 1 stock cube (or 1 teaspoon stock powder) into 1 cup (250ml) water to make 1 cup of stock. If you prefer to make your own fresh stock, see recipes on page 111.

SUGAR we used coarse, granulated table sugar, also known as crystal sugar, unless otherwise specified.
Brown an extremely soft, fine granulated sugar retaining molasses for its characteristic deep colour and flavour.
Caster also known as superfine or finely granulated table sugar.
Icing sugar mixture also known as confectioners' sugar or powdered sugar; granulated sugar crushed together with a small amount (about 3%) of cornflour added.
Palm very fine sugar from the coconut palm. It is usually sold in compressed cakes. Also known as *gula*

corn tortilla

flour tortilla

jawa, gula melaka and *jaggery*. Brown or black sugar can be substituted.
Raw natural brown granulated sugar.

SUMAC a purple-red and astringent spice ground from the berries of shrubs that flourish wild around the Mediterranean; adds a tart, lemony flavour to dips and dressings and goes well with barbecued meat.

TAHINI a rich, buttery paste made from crushed sesame seeds; used in making hummus and other Middle-Eastern sauces.

TAT SOI (rosette pak choy, *tai gu choy*, Chinese flat cabbage) a variety of bok choy, developed to grow close to the ground so it is easily protected from frost.

TOMATO
Paste triple-concentrated tomato puree used to add flavour to soups, stews, sauces and casseroles.
Sauce also known as ketchup or catsup; a condiment made from slow-cooked tomatoes, vinegar and spices.

TORTILLA thin, round unleavened bread originating in Mexico; can be made at home or purchased frozen, fresh or vacuum-packed. Two kinds are available, one made from wheat flour and the other from corn (maize meal).

TURNIP a round, white-fleshed root vegetable. Used in soups and stews.

spinach

baby spinach

watercress

rocket

WASABI an Asian horseradish used to make a fiery sauce traditionally served in small amounts with Japanese raw fish dishes.

WATER CHESTNUTS resemble chestnuts in appearance, hence the English name. They are small brown tubers with a crisp, white, nutty-tasting flesh. Their crunchy texture is best experienced fresh, however, canned and frozen water chestnuts are more easily obtained.

WATERCRESS small, crisp, deep-green, rounded leaves having a slightly bitter, peppery flavour. Good in salads, soups and as an ingredient in sandwiches.

WINE the adage is that you should never cook with wine you wouldn't drink; we used good-quality dry white and red wines in our recipes.

YEAST a 7g (1/4oz) sachet of dried yeast (2 teaspoons) is equal to 15g (1/2oz) compressed yeast if you are substituting one type for the other.

YOGURT plain, unflavoured yogurt – in addition to being good eaten on its own – can be used as a meat tenderiser, as the basis for various sauces and dips or as an enricher and thickener.

ZUCCHINI also known in recipes as courgette.

INDEX

MAKE YOUR OWN STOCK

These recipes can be made up to 4 days ahead and stored, covered, in the refrigerator. Be sure to remove any fat from the surface after the cooled stock has been refrigerated overnight. If the stock is to be kept longer, it is best to freeze it in smaller quantities.

Stock is also available in cans or tetra packs. Stock cubes or powder can be used. As a guide, 1 teaspoon of stock powder or 1 small crumbled stock cube mixed with 1 cup (250ml) water will give a fairly strong stock. Be aware of the salt and fat content of stock cubes and powders and prepared stocks.

All stock recipes make about 2.5 litres (10 cups).

BEEF STOCK

2kg meaty beef bones
2 medium (300g) onions
2 sticks celery, chopped
2 medium (250g) carrots, chopped
3 bay leaves
2 teaspoons black peppercorns
5 litres (20 cups) water
3 litres (12 cups) water, extra

Place bones and unpeeled chopped onions in baking dish. Bake in hot oven about 1 hour or until bones and onions are well browned. Transfer bones and onions to large pan, add celery, carrots, bay leaves, peppercorns and water, simmer, uncovered, 3 hours. Add extra water, simmer, uncovered, further 1 hour; strain.

CHICKEN STOCK

2kg chicken bones
2 medium (300g) onions, chopped
2 sticks celery, chopped
2 medium (250g) carrots, chopped
3 bay leaves
2 teaspoons black peppercorns
5 litres (20 cups) water

Combine all ingredients in large pan, simmer, uncovered, 2 hours; strain.

FISH STOCK

1.5kg fish bones
3 litres (12 cups) water
1 medium (150g) onion, chopped
2 sticks celery, chopped
2 bay leaves
1 teaspoon black peppercorns

Combine all ingredients in large pan, simmer, uncovered, 20 minutes; strain.

VEGETABLE STOCK

2 large (360g) carrots, chopped
2 large (360g) parsnips, chopped
4 medium (600g) onions, chopped
12 sticks celery, chopped
4 bay leaves
2 teaspoons black peppercorns
6 litres (24 cups) water

Combine all ingredients in large pan, simmer, uncovered, 1 1/2 hours; strain.

FACTS AND FIGURES

Wherever you live, you'll be able to use our recipes with the help of these easy-to-follow conversions. While these conversions are approximate only, the difference between an exact and the approximate conversion of various liquid and dry measures is but minimal and will not affect your cooking results.

DRY MEASURES

Metric	Imperial
15g	1/2oz
30g	1oz
60g	2oz
90g	3oz
125g	4oz (1/4lb)
155g	5oz
185g	6oz
220g	7oz
250g	8oz (1/2lb)
280g	9oz
315g	10oz
345g	11oz
375g	12oz (3/4lb)
410g	13oz
440g	14oz
470g	15oz
500g	16oz (1lb)
750g	24oz (11/2lb)
1kg	32oz (2lb)

LIQUID MEASURES

Metric	Imperial
30ml	1 fluid oz
60ml	2 fluid oz
100ml	3 fluid oz
125ml	4 fluid oz
150ml	5 fluid oz (1/4 pint/1 gill)
190ml	6 fluid oz
250ml	8 fluid oz
300ml	10 fluid oz (1/2 pint)
500ml	16 fluid oz
600ml	20 fluid oz (1 pint)
1000ml (1 litre)	13/4 pints

HELPFUL MEASURES

Metric	Imperial
3mm	1/8in
6mm	1/4in
1cm	1/2in
2cm	3/4in
2.5cm	1in
5cm	2in
6cm	21/2in
8cm	3in
10cm	4in
13cm	5in
15cm	6in
18cm	7in
20cm	8in
23cm	9in
25cm	10in
28cm	11in
30cm	12in (1ft)

MEASURING EQUIPMENT

The difference between one country's measuring cups and another's is, at most, within a 2 or 3 teaspoon variance. (For the record, 1 Australian metric measuring cup holds approximately 250ml.) The most accurate way of measuring dry ingredients is to weigh them. When measuring liquids, use a clear glass or plastic jug with the metric markings.

If you would like to purchase The Australian Women's Weekly Test Kitchen's metric measuring cups and spoons (as approved by Standards Australia), turn to page 120 for details and order coupon. You will receive:

- a graduated set of 4 cups for measuring dry ingredients, with sizes marked on the cups.
- a graduated set of 4 spoons for measuring dry and liquid ingredients, with amounts marked on the spoons.
- 1 teaspoon: 5ml.
- 1 tablespoon: 20ml.

Note: North America and UK use 15ml tablespoons. All cup and spoon measurements are level.

How To Measure

When using graduated metric measuring cups, shake dry ingredients loosely into the appropriate cup. Do not tap the cup on a bench or tightly pack the ingredients unless directed to do so. Level top of measuring cups and measuring spoons with a knife. When measuring liquids, place a clear glass or plastic jug with metric markings on a flat surface to check accuracy at eye level.

We use large eggs having an average weight of 60g.

OVEN TEMPERATURES

These oven temperatures are only a guide. Always check the manufacturer's manual.

	C° (Celsius)	F° (Fahrenheit)	Gas Mark
Very slow	120	250	1
Slow	150	300	2
Moderately slow	160	325	3
Moderate	180 - 190	350 - 375	4
Moderately hot	200 - 210	400 - 425	5
Hot	220 - 230	450 - 475	6
Very hot	240 - 250	500 - 525	7

Life's easier with these great Home Library gifts

Protect your favourite cookbooks and keep them clean, tidy and within easy reach with this smart vinyl folder. PLUS you can follow our recipes perfectly with a set of measuring cups and spoons, as used in the Women's Weekly Test Kitchen.

TO ORDER YOUR BOOK HOLDER OR MEASURING SET:

Price: Book Holder $11.95 (Australia); elsewhere $A21.95.
Metric Measuring Set $5.95 (Australia); $8.00 (New Zealand); $A9.95 elsewhere
prices include postage and handling. This offer is available in all countries.

Phone: Have your credit card details ready. Sydney: (02) 9260 0035; **elsewhere in Australia:** 1800 252 515 (free call, Mon-Fri, 8.30am-5.30pm) or FAX your order to (02) 9267 4363 or MAIL your order by photocopying or completing the coupon below.

Payment: **Australian residents:** we accept the credit cards listed, money orders and cheques. **Overseas residents:** we accept the credit cards listed, drafts in $A drawn on an Australian bank, and also British, New Zealand and U.S. cheques in the currency of the country of issue. Credit card charges are at the exchange rate current at the time of payment.

Complete coupon and fax or post to:
AWW Home Library Reader Offer, ACP Direct, PO Box 7036, Sydney NSW 1028.

❏ **Metric Measuring Set**   ❏ **Holder**
Please indicate number(s) required.

Mr/Mrs/Ms _____

Address _____

_____

Postcode _____ Country _____

Ph: Bus. Hours:( ) _____

I enclose my cheque/money order for $ _____ payable to ACP Direct
OR: please charge my:

❏ Bankcard ❏ Visa ❏ MasterCard ❏ Diners Club ❏ Amex

❏❏❏❏ ❏❏❏❏ ❏❏❏❏ ❏❏❏❏ ❏❏❏❏

Expiry Date ____/____

Cardholder's signature _____

(Please allow up to 30 days for delivery within Australia. Allow up to 6 weeks for overseas deliveries.) Both offers expire 30/6/99.   HLEBBQ98